TIGER STRIPES

A MEMOIR

HANNAH RENAE

HURN
PUBLICATIONS

DEDICATION

For my mother—there wasn't a parenting book in the world that could have prepared you for me, but you have loved me unconditionally through it all. You have been a rock for me through everything and I am so grateful for you,

Hayden—you are my biggest reason to keep fighting. Always be kind and always follow your dreams. I love you with all of my heart.

and

Henry—these words would not exist without you. Thank you for giving me a chance at life and at my dreams. You've kept me going on my worst days, and you make the good ones all the more beautiful. You inspire me every day. I love you.

In loving memory of Carissa and Zachary Cloe

THE LETTER H

October 7, 2019

"HENRY! HENRY! HENNN-RYYYY!!!!"

I am screaming at the top of my lungs and can feel my throat tearing, becoming raw. I don't know how many times I have said his name now, but it is all I know how to do because nothing is making any sense.

I am in a locked room and flashes of images are going through my head, but there is only one thing, one thought that I can focus on, that is pounding through my brain throughout this confusion and that is pouring out of my lungs to the point that my chest feels like it is going to rip.

"HENRY!" I choke on his name and a sob.

He cannot hear me, and he is not coming. He doesn't know where I am and I don't know where I am, but I know I am not supposed to be here—and I have to get out.

I beat at the metal door that barricades me from something unknown and choke on words that begin with H.

"HENRY!" "

"HELP!"

"HENRY!"

"HELP!"

I repeat these words for what feels like a lifetime, until I forget how to speak and my begging turns to carnal screaming —shrieking.

No one comes. No one answers. I wait for footsteps, for the sound of the door unlocking, but all I can hear is the sound of my frantic breaths and the echoes of a lamentation that is anything but human.

I look down at my body. My feet are bare against the concrete floor; I cannot feel them. The jean shorts I am wearing show off my slender, scratched legs and remind me that I am small and feeble at this moment, but in an act of desperation, I put all of my faith in the power of momentum and I run. I fucking run as fast as I can from the three paces it takes to get from the wall to the ominous looming, locked door and attack it with my entire being, letting out my most vicious battle cry as I fumble towards it.

The door wins.

I try again.

And again.

And again.

And again.

And again.

I am degraded to a crumbling, bruised ball of flesh.

I can barely speak, my throat reduced to sandpaper.

Everything hurts and I can taste the bitterness of blood in my mouth. The floor is like ice against my bare legs. Through the tears in my eyes I see the moon shining through a window at the top of the room. It is full and brilliant and illuminates the white of the brick walls that surround me. I realize that there is writing on them. People have been here before me. People will be here after me. Why am I here though? I should not be.

I should be home, where I belong. In bed, with him. *Safe*. I feel anything but that word in this moment, as terror sweeps through every single one of my nerves.

I whisper in one last futile attempt:

"Henry?"

But there is silence. Horrible, deafening, fatal silence.

And it seems to last forever, until I hear it, or think I do. A click, the door unlocking, and the small room is suddenly filled with light. Fluorescence suffocates me.

When I dare to open my eyes, they do not find Henry. Instead I find a police officer looking back at me. He wears broad, black framed glasses that are too big for his face and he looks eerily familiar. A sudden memory of lying in a hospital bed comes to me but does not fully resonate. His face is forlorn and almost disappointed, as if he expected more out of me.

"I thought you were going to hurt yourself," he tells me. "Promise you'll stay calm and you can come out for a bit. We've got to get you fingerprinted."

It's then that I have the shattering realization that I am drunk and in a holding cell at a police station. The reason why escapes me though, as I try to grab onto flashes of sober memories but drown in my current state-of-mind.

I try to breathe with intent as I remember every single arrest-cliché in the book, and I cling to the fact that I am going to get my phone call. They will probably let me go—they have to. If anything, they will make me stay the night at the most.

I remember the silent promise I had once made myself— that the moment I got a DUI that I would put down the bottle for good. Jail was the worst it could get. It had been my crowning achievement at my last three rehabs that I had never graced the inside of a jail cell and I never planned to.

"Continue down the path you have been," one of the staff members at my second treatment center had told me after sharing her own story about prison, "and jail is a guarantee."

And here I am. Her words have come to pass, as promised.

I then remember what else she told me as we talked over a pack of Marlboro Reds on a warm Orange County night.

"Finish the 90 days," she had said, "Or you will not make it and there will come a day where you will no longer be able to cry out 'I'm a good person!'. You will lie. You will steal. You will become someone and something else. You will hurt everyone you love. You will lose everything, and just when you think you have lost it all, you will lose something else."

In this moment of scathing loneliness and terror, it seems the day of reckoning has come. I know not what awaits me or what I have left. I don't know what I have done, but I know it is bad and that I will not be going home tonight, as the police inform me that I will be going to the county's main women's jail in Lynwood. I ask the officer where that is.

"Near Compton," is all he says.

I choke on my own saliva as I contemplate what I am going into, and still: *why, why, why?* What on earth have I done?

The glasses-clad officer gives me a sorry smirk as he asks me to put my hands behind my back and says, "I'm going to have to put these on tight since you slipped out of the ones you were in earlier."

I can feel my jaw drop and then tighten.

This does not sound like me. It couldn't be me. Then I think of the glaring and painful abrasions on my left wrist and realize he is right. I meekly put my hands behind my back and allow him to tighten the cuffs and wince as the cold, harsh metal cuts into my open flesh.

Passing minutes would turn into hours, would turn into days; time became a figment of the extraordinary as every second manifested as a year. No one was coming to save me, and I was very quickly to learn that "get out of jail free" cards don't exist. I had made my bed: it was time to lay in it or hang myself with the sheet. I was about to learn just how thick brick walls could be, and how I would have to break free of the prison that was me to ever truly be free.

But I'm getting ahead of myself...

PART I
THE BLOODBATH

CADILLAC PROBLEMS

March 7, 2019

I stare at the project I have been avoiding. I'll get to it; I always get to it. Whether it's in an hour or this weekend, it will get done. I am good at my job and I make things happen, but it's Friday and to me that is some sort of finish line. As I read over the essay-of-an-email from my client about everything she wants included in an upcoming press release, I know I should really get started. Instead, I decide to head to the other side of the office and think of some sort of excuse to see him—Henry.

I look good today. As of late, I always make sure I look good when I know he is going to be here. Nonetheless I tidy and straighten myself up and quickly touch up my candy pink lipstick. I can see my coworker rolling her eyes behind me. She knows where I am going. This little secret may be hidden with words, but the red my cheeks turns when he looks at me doesn't lie.

Yet before I cross to make my way to his office, my confidence faulters. For what reason I cannot say—it's been months, this thing between him and I, because there really is no name for it. We work, we rendezvous, and we have our not so little secret that exists beyond the walls of this office. I haven't seen him today, and I need him to see me—take notice, but I need some ferocity first, so I head to my car.

As I walk down the stairs to the car lot, I ponder the time —it's almost noon and I hope he doesn't decide now is a good time to take lunch or leave for the day. I begin to hurry and pull out my keys, deciding to move my car for the second time in the day to pretend I am actually doing something. Once in my car, I immediately fumble for the coffee tumbler I have stuck in the driver's door, my nerves calming as I hear the liquid inside sloshing against the metal. I take a quick look to ensure none of my colleagues are watching and down five quick gulps as I clumsily turn on the car and reverse. My eyes search the lot for another open space and of course there is only one—next to him.

I repark the car and contemplate the shining silver of his Cadillac as I take a few more sips of warm whiskey. It beams in the sunlight. This car represents something to me—it symbolizes the freedom of life I have a few times a week, it represents me getting what I want, it is a flag that I break the rules—and I like it. I take one more sip, and with it a deep breath, it's showtime. I return to the office with a new sense of confidence.

I feel like the most important person in the room as the bottom of my boots make a pronouncing clack and I glide across the floor and to my computer for a quick glance. When I look at it, I find that in my absence, he's beat me to the punch.

Come in, a message from him reads on my screen. It's always those two words and they always make my heart start beating faster.

In a panic, I pick up anything I can use from my desk as a shield to hide any sense of insecurity he may see. I fill my hands with two notebooks and a pen before I make my way briskly to his office and announce my arrival in his doorway with a light knock and a shy smile. To announce that this is our domain, I shut the door behind me. As I situate myself in the leather chair opposite of him, I try to look at ease as he scans me with his eyes.

It's the one thing I've never been able to stop coming undone from—his stare. His soft, but sharp brown eyes speak and see through me.

"How's it going?" he asks in a casual tone.

"Good, almost done with the press release," I lie.

"That's great," he says with his notorious smirk. "Send it to me when you're done."

I nod, barely understanding the request. Instead having an entire conversation with him with our eyes alone. We will be seeing each other tonight, no question of that. I get lost in the thought of what that might mean, as this man never fails to surprise or satisfy me.

"Here's your check," he says and as he slaps it on the table I am stung back into reality.

It's payday, and the same man who pays me is the same one I will be spending the night with—and I don't feel bad about it. Not at all.

I smile and thank him, shooting him one last sly smile as I leave, and return to my desk to wait. I wait and wait and wait until the clock nears 4 PM, the time he leaves. I've busied the time with menial tasks, mindless banter with coworkers, and a trip to the liquor store. My pressing project is still not complete, let alone started, but like I said, it will get done.

Has he left? I wonder, looking at the clock and thinking of an excuse to go by his office again without making my affections look obvious, but then my phone buzzes.

I want to go to Vegas, it says.

Lol, I reply. *We should sometime! We hanging out tonight?*

I'm going, he says, *if you want to come, I'm leaving in 45.*

I don't even think. I shut my computer and begin to pack my things. I am supposed to be here for another two hours, but I don't care, and I don't explain myself to anyone.

This is not me. I am a planner—I like to know what is happening, when, why, and how, far before it does, but Henry brings something out in me I have never known before. Something that says no to all of my normal instincts and makes me just want to be alive. He makes me abandon thoughts and reservations and just become. So, I go.

Before I even clock out, I am on the phone with him.

"Yeah I will go," I say casually. "But I need to get my things together."

"Well you better be ready in 45 minutes, because that's when I am going."

"I need time to pack," I begin.

"You can get stuff there," he stops me.

Henry doesn't take excuses; if I want to go, I'll be ready when he says—and I am going.

"Okay," I say. "See you then."

Then begins a frantic rush as I contemplate all I will need to do in less than an hour—get back to my house, pack, and, most importantly, go to the liquor store, again—because it's a long drive to Vegas.

I call my mother and inform her of my plans, feigning that the trip is work-related. I think I even try to convince myself of this as I try to arrange her keeping Hayden, my five-year-old son, for extra time so I can make this happen. By her tone, it's clear she doesn't believe me, but it doesn't matter. I mute the phone as I purchase two small bottles of whiskey, and by the time I am home I have downed a quarter of one.

I pack the essentials first—the two bottles I just bought

and my pills. I then hurriedly create a pile of dresses, under-garments, shoes, and other items I think will be appropriate for the trip, but I have resigned myself to the idea of "I'll just get what I need there."

Before I know it, my knight in his shining Cadillac has arrived and I realize that I am not prepared whatsoever. Yet as I shuffle with my bags to the car and he steps out and looks at me, any misgivings and all tension is gone. He's here, I'm here, and we're going—to hell with the rest of them.

We drive away from it all and music washes over my ears. I am entranced with him and this moment and then it all becomes dark and I sleep.

When I awake, it is to the glimmering of bright lights and a valet.

"Come on, Hannah," Henry says, irritation seething in his tone.

We're here? I wonder. How could I have possibly slept through the entire ride? But the pounding in my head gives me all the answer I need.

Disoriented, I try to collect myself as quick as possible, but I practically fall out of the car as I try to figure out what hotel we are at. By some miracle, he is completely distracted talking to the valet and doesn't see the calamity that is me. I begin to multitask—unloading my bags from the car and slipping one of the whiskey bottles into my purse.

The next several minutes feel like a disaster and I am met with his singular impatience and infuriation—the feeling of dread and panic it instills in me is almost as powerful as the ecstasy he can evoke from me. Yet like it always does, in a moment it is washed away. We are suddenly walking through the lobby, the tautness between us relinquishing by the

second, and we are heading exactly where I need to go
—the bar.

He lights both of us a cigarette as I impatiently wait for
our drinks, when they come I exchange him his drink for a
smoke and we clink our plastic cups to absolutely nothing at
all, other than the fact that we together, here, free from it all—
at least for now. It's another ocular conversation, but it is
enough.

I inhale cigarette smoke between harsh sips of bourbon
and feel everything melt away and I look at him with complete
revere and he looks back at me with his signature smile—
there is nothing perfect or normal about this, but it is mine,
and for this time, he is mine and I feel like the most important
person in the room.

"Ready?" Henry asks.

And I nod, I am ready for absolutely anything.

RED MEANS DEAD

April 8, 2019

My eyes are searching for something, anything to grab onto, but all I can see is the bottom of a porcelain tub and murky clouds of crimson. *Blood.* My blood. I need air and I need it now, but the crushing force from the hand on the back of my neck tells me I will not be getting it anytime soon.

I came here to be free, and instead I am going to die at the bottom of a rusting, rotting motel bathtub. Alone, except for the company of my killer. I wait for the water to fill my lungs, my body, my life. I wait.

"Mam?"

I hear the voice. It is clear, but far away.

"Mam!"

My eyes shoot open and I immediately swat at the hand shaking me.

"Sorry to startle you," says the kind-eyed stewardess, who is clearly startled herself. "We are about to make our descent and all tray tables need to be put up and secured."

I say nothing, but nod, barely understanding the request. I curse myself for falling asleep and try to discern nightmares from reality.

Looking out the window, I feel a small sense of calm as I see the concrete and glass postcard view that is Los Angeles from the clouds. It isn't trees and it isn't mountains, and for that I am grateful, but any semblance of peace is quickly replaced by terror as I become aware of my ever-present shaking hands and begin the frantic search for what I need to hold me over. I'm so close. It's been six days. Six agonizing days, and I will not let my journey be ruined now by a breakdown.

I frantically finger through my bag until the pulsating in my chest is soothed by the clacking of pills against plastic. After doing a mental calculation of LA traffic in my head, I deduce that I will probably be getting what I need in about two, two-and-a-half hours, and I should only need one to hold me over, but instead I take three.

Within a few minutes the plane is breaching the runway and lands with an ominous thud, bouncing about the landing strip, as if to announce the chaos that is me has returned home.

This wasn't supposed to happen. None of it was. Like a lot of other things in my life as of late, my second trip to America's final, frozen frontier began with a few swigs of warm Jack Daniel's and a bright idea. Everyone else could think I was mad, but in reality, I was an adventurer, vicious for escape from the consuming Los Angeles smog with its high-rise buildings and presumptuous folk. None of that was for me—Alaska was, with its picturesque mountains, leaping fish, and endless skies. I would finally be as free as a bird.

The first time I had made a descent into the 49th state I had a window seat, so I had asked for one this time too. That first Alaskan view was of the most massive mound of ice and rock I could have ever believed existed, contrasted only by the burgeoning yellow of the spruce trees that sprayed in the wind and shined in the fall sun. It was a new world with its own song, and I wanted to be a part of it.

Two years later I arrived at the end of a long winter and in the black of night. Not a glacier, tree, or sign of life in sight. It was an omen that I couldn't feel or see.

I barely made it onto that flight. And in the coming months I would look back and ask myself so many times what would have happened if I had not. Would any of this had ended differently? No one will know, but I will always wonder.

I left Alaska running, hoping and thinking to never look back, but the darkness that I descended into, was only a taste of what was to come.

It's 6:42 AM and I am in Los Angeles and not Alaska, but my phone buzzes and the sender, Zak, my brother, quickly reminds me that I just was.

You ok? It reads. I can hear him asking the question.

Absolutely not. I am anything but okay.

Yes, I respond, *I'm fine, just landed.*

Just don't drink again! Otherwise you will start all over.

Yeah, I know.

I know is what I say and what I think, but what he and everyone else doesn't know is there is not a damn thing in this world that can stop me from a drink right now, because I don't care about having another seizure, I don't care about how bad my body still throbs, I don't care about hurting more people, or hurting myself, I care about silencing the agony in my head, and I am so close to it.

As I walk towards the baggage claim I debate even reclaiming my things. They are just reminders. They are just more to bring, more to carry, and more time wasted.

Walking through the people a sudden feeling of panging, stabbing emptiness hits me though, and I instinctually clutch then scratch at the flesh on my lower abdomen. It is empty; I am empty, and I think of Henry. *Henry*. For the most fleeting second I debate abandoning my mission to self-destruct, to die, and just going to him. Because sitting in that cold, lonely Alaskan bedroom, hidden away at the end of the world, I wept so many tears for the things I could not have, and so many of those tears were for him. But I couldn't tell him over the past six days over the phone, so how was I going to tell him now to his face? It was a nice thought, a nice dream, but it would not be happening today, or anytime soon.

I couldn't tell Henry, because who knew what he would say. After all, what could he? What I did know though, was that whiskey had never judged me.

As I sit in the back of an Uber in bumper-to-bumper Los Angeles traffic, I try to soothe the throbbing in my head by kneading at my temples. Just a few days prior I had a gun loaded, safety-off, my hand on the trigger, ready to fire to one of them.

Carrie, my brother's wife, had been struck with a debilitating migraine headache and he had to take her to the ER. I was to be left at the house, but not unprotected. A lot had just happened after all, and anything else *could* happen.

"Listen for the dogs," Zak told me, "They'll bark if anyone is coming down the driveway."

"And here," he had said, as he handed me a matte black pistol and flipped a switch on it illuminating a red light. "Hopefully you won't have to use it, but if you do, you know how to shoot, and remember—red means dead."

I didn't have to shoot anyone or anything that day. Yet as I sat with myself at the end of the world, reflecting on the horrors that had just occurred, I wanted so badly for it all to just end. I sobbed as I felt the metal barrel cool against my skin as I held the gun with a shaking hand.

And I dropped it—because as much as I wanted to die, I couldn't bear the thought of my brother, who had just saved my life, coming home to my brain matter splattered all over the floor.

No, if I was going to die, it would be on my own accord and back home—if I ever got back home.

I think there was a part of me that day that had hoped that the Man with the Red Hair would show up, so that I could shoot him and get all my pain out of what he had did to me one bullet at a time. I would shoot him until I was out of ammunition and then I would smash his blue eyes in with my steel-toed boots.

Who was I? I didn't think thoughts like this, not ever.

But the truth was, that if *He* came down that driveway, he would easily shoot and kill me first. My shot was shaky and mediocre at best, and despite looking compact, the pistol was heavy. If *He* arrived, I was done for. His red hair would mean death or worse—but I would make sure that would never happen. Not again.

Now here I was, back in LA—as though I had entered a different universe, but with the same mindset. I could follow through on whatever I wanted now, but the first thing I needed was a drink, so I could not think about that, and think about what my future looked like. If I even had one.

We make our way through downtown and eventually the driver takes a shortcut and hops onto Route 66. The dry foothills with their patches of artificial-looking green give me some semblance of peace. They are not black mountaintops capped in snow and they do not tower so high that they make me feel like an ant.

I feel a wetness between my legs and shift in my seat.

All I can think is— *fuck*. More blood. Will it ever stop? Probably not, as I am almost sure at this point that God is punishing me for something. I want to scream at the driver to step on it, but if he did, we would just slam into the lines of cars in front of us.

After the longest two hours of my life, I am finally at the liquor store and the face of my familiar cashier brings a genuine smile to my face, but I cut the small talk and get what I need. I buy two bottles of wine and a fifth of whiskey, because I don't know how long I will be in my room for, but I want oblivion and I want it now.

My driver finally drops me off at my home, and I dump my mess of luggage into a pile in the living room, or what is visible of it. There is a mess off clothes, children's toys, books, and sheets of random paper everywhere. I shed my jacket and change into a pair of musty smelling pajamas while simultaneously unscrewing one of the bottles of Cabernet.

I make no effort to tell anyone I am home, to greet my landlady, check on my son, or go to Henry. I don't even bother to go get myself a glass. I take five long pulls straight from the bottle and wait for the feeling of numbness to wash into me, and as I drink more, it does.

At some point I awake from a black void into the dead of night and search for my light switch in a half-drunken haze. When I find and flip it on, yellow fluorescence floods the room and makes me wince and charge from my bedroom into the living room. In the dark, my hands search for the bottle of whiskey and I take an unmeasured shot to balance myself out. Next to it I feel and find my phone. Five new notifications.

Mom.

Dad.

Henry.

Zak.

And a voicemail from a 907 area-code number. *Wasilla, Alaska.* Probably a detective or trooper, but I have no interest in any of that now. They can't help me, *but this can,* I think, as I take a sip of warm Jack Daniel's.

I set my phone down and return to my bedroom, my eyes more adjusted. I see it right away. Blaring like a mockery on my pink bed sheets—a massive red stain, and I look down at my legs. More blood indeed.

I rush back to my phone and check the time. It's 1-something and I know no one is up. Except…

Alex. My ex-insomniac.

Call Henry, something inside me is screaming, but I don't have anything to say to him. How am I going to explain this? Yet I know if I call, he will answer. If I go to his house now, he will open the door and let me in, and I can stop all of this. But before I can think any more on it, my fingers are dialing the memorized movements of Alex's phone number.

He picks up on the second ring.

"What?" he says. He's drunk too.

"I was just in Alaska," I blurt out.

"What?" he says and then he laughs. He had gone with me on my last trip and it had been a whirlwind of fighting, drinking, and sightseeing.

"It didn't go well." I say, "Something happened with…"

When I say the name, I am met with silence on the other end, as if I don't have to explain more.

"Can I come over?" I ask.

"I guess."

He sends me his new address. I haven't been to his new

place since he moved out of our old house, but it is near the college.

I find a small duffel bag and pack a few items into it. I have no interest in coming back to this place anytime soon.

By some miracle, I make it down the freeway and to Alex's apartment and stumble up the stairs with my half-empty bottle of whiskey. I knock on the door. No answer. Knock again. I search for my phone amongst my bags, cursing at Alex under my breath the entire time, until I finally find it and realize the nature of my predicament.

212. This is 216. I hurry down the corridor before an angry group of college students has the chance to call the police and Alex is already in the doorway, waiting.

"Nice," is all he says.

"Fuck you," I respond and throw the mess of my belongings onto the living room floor with a complete absence of courtesy.

"Sit," he commands, motioning to the corduroy couch that looks like it was found on the side of the road, but I do. "What happened?"

I want to tell him. I even try to tell him, but the right words don't exist within me, and every time I try to explain, I just see pictures in my brain and hear deafening sounds in my ears. At some point I fall asleep on the floor.

When I awake, we waste no time making a trek to the liquor store and I can't stop crying.

Three more missed calls from a 907 number. Four from Zak. One from Henry. I should probably check in, but I need to do this first.

When we get back, I scoff at his living space. It is small, dim and depressing. A twin bed, that looks something like a barracks bunk is in the corner with a sad bundle of flannel sheets. His desk is stained in red wine and piles books and graph paper are the only décor.

"You live here?"

He looks insulted.

"It's temporary," he retorts, "You left, remember? I wasn't exactly going to keep a two-bedroom place all for myself. I don't take up much room."

His false modesty makes me want to vomit and I begin punching in a messy text to Henry on my phone and stop. Again, what is there to say?

That morning the bright red blood has finally stopped, but my head has not, and I am wishing more than ever that I had pulled that fateful trigger, but here I am.

IF YOU PULL THE PIN TO A GRENADE, DON'T BE SURPRISED WHEN IT BLOWS UP IN YOUR FACE

April 13, 2019

I am on a mission. It involves getting from the front door to the trunk of my car and Henry not noticing a thing. It's 8:00 AM.

"I need to get something from my car," I say, already in motion.

"Wait," he starts, but I've started, and nothing is stopping me.

"I'll be right back," I snap.

Now I know he's watching so I have to be careful, make it look like I actually have something I am doing.

I practically sprint across the street and arrive at my trunk, filled with relief as it pops, and I see the glimmering of the glass bottle. I promptly shove it into a bag which I try to conceal with my body as I make my way to the front seat and duck, praying Henry isn't looking. Unscrewing the cap, I stare in dismay with the realization that I am going to need find a way to get more and soon, but I duck my head and partake in what is there.

The chardonnay is warm and sour from being open all night, but I fight past the putrid taste as I hone in on the relief it fills me with in each sip.

One.

Two.

Three.

Four.

Five.

There's a quarter of the bottle left, and I am feeling better, but when will I be able to come outside again? When will I be able to get more? With those questions in mind, I don't hesitate as I down the rest and stash the bottle underneath the passenger seat, hiding it with the collection of trash that has formed over the past several weeks. Better safe than sorry.

I return to the house and avoid Henry's gaze as I make my way straight to the kitchen to consume something, anything, to wash the vile, rotting taste out of my mouth that will give me away. My head is spinning, and I feel on the verge of retching, but I try to drown the feeling in gulps of an energy drink.

He's in the doorway.

"Can we talk?" he asks.

"I need to get ready for work," I say, wiping my mouth and avoiding the question.

"You're not going to work," he says. His tone is firm and final.

I just stare at him and make my way to the couch in silence. Defeat of every kind washes over me. I am in no mood or place to argue; I am exhausted.

"What." I say, not ask.

"I think you should get some help," he says.

"What do you mean?" I ask, as if I have no idea what he is talking about.

"The drinking, Hannah," he pauses and looks at me with his big brown eyes, kind, but concerned. "It's getting out of control."

I stare at him. What does he mean by "help"? Then it hits me.

"I. Am. Not. Going. To. Rehab." I say and get up from the couch. Now I am angry.

He grabs my hand, sits me back down, and smiles.

~

April 17, 2019

I am 21 years old, the legal drinking age, and on my way to get medically detoxed from alcohol. I've decided that the entire ordeal is dramatic and over-the-top, but I have obliged out of the desperate relief from the chaos and Henry's knack for coercion.

When we arrive at the hospital, I am overwhelmed by the massive white structure that is Huntington Memorial Hospital. It's one of the biggest and most beautiful hospitals I have ever seen, and I feel so small standing at its entrance, my head spinning with the whiskey I drank on the way.

My head grows dizzy as I scan the building, so I focus my attention on Henry who seems to immediately recognize the flash of blonde hair coming towards us, even though he has never met her. My mother. A wave of seething irritation courses through my veins as she saunters up and Henry introduces himself to her as I light a cigarette and retreat behind a pillar. So much for meet the parents.

I don't see the people, I am too busy thinking on other things, but in the back of my mind, I know that they see me.

Watching my mother and Henry talking makes me want to scream; I fight to hold back the compulsive need to shriek by swallowing stale cigarette smoke.

I want to go home, but where is that? What is that? Who

is that? I don't belong here, but I don't think I really belong anywhere else either. I want a drink.

My mother approaches me and begins to say something, but I walk past her and to the only person I can see. *Henry.*

Nothing makes any sense. I don't know why I am here. I just know that they think I am sick, and I have drank an obscene amount over the past four days. He is going to be gone soon, going to go home, back to the place where I have left a mess and I have the sudden feeling of utter panic. I love this man. I love him so, so much. A wave of memories flashes through my intoxicated mind.

I was engaged to be wed and had been searching for work fervently since my fiancée, my son, and I had moved from Santa Barbara to the Greater Los Angeles area after my graduation. It was a slow process. To try and soothe my isolation and ever-increasing depression my fiancée had gifted me with a German Shepherd puppy. My days went from constant studying, beach runs, writing, and talks with the academic elite to cleaning up after a 25-year old man and a 3-year old boy's messes, runs with the dog, drop-offs to and from Hayden's preschool, reruns of *Paw Patrol*, infinite job applications, and, most of all, increasing amounts of Cabernet Sauvignon.

While I used to simply toss out the remainder of whatever Alex had not finished the night before, I began pouring the remainder into a tall glass before he got home that night with more bottles for himself.

After months, it looked like a well-paying job opportunity was finally on the horizon. I had been to an abundance of interviews for jobs that I did not want and didn't feel pressed to take them. We were financially alright; I wanted to work for stimulation—and managing apartment complexes or being an administrator at the local college was not going to do that for me. A job eventually came along that paid well and allowed me to be creative, was close enough to home, and, most importantly, didn't involve me interacting with many people.

"I'll need you to travel with me a couple times a month," my new potential boss told me after offering me the job, and it was over.

I was a mother, and almost a wife. I had a family to take care of. Jetting off to New York didn't fit into that. I was ready to give up and had one last interview scheduled for a copy-writing position that I had sought after.

I had donned my black dress pants and blazer and arranged my brown hair in loose curls to one side of my head. The office was close to home, the pay wasn't great, and when I entered the workspace, I was somewhat alarmed that not a single person looked up from their computer to welcome me or acknowledge my existence. Until he emerged.

Bright-eyed and with a beaming smile he introduced himself as "Henry". He was dressed casually, but his essence was cool and collected to a tee. While I was always nervous in an interview, he was easy to talk to, and sat comfortably while he asked me about my experience, my goals, and my life. I liked him. I wanted to work for him, and within a day I had an offer and I was ready to start immediately.

Before my first day I sent him a barrage of emails, thanking him for the opportunity, asking things like:

"Hi Henry! Before Monday, I wanted to check with you about the dress code policy. I kind of got an idea while being there, but I just wanted to clarify. Best, Hannah"

He told me casual, but from the get-go something about this man made me always want to be exceptional.

I started the following Monday and the man with the sentence-stopping smile was seldom found in that time. I heard rumors. He liked to travel, would sometimes be gone weeks, even months at a time—Vegas and Chicago were apparently frequented. I wondered if he had a wife, or a girlfriend, or women who waited for him in the unknown places he went. It became a mystery that intrigued me. I wanted to know him, and I didn't know why.

Now here we were, Henry and I, almost a year from my interview. At some point along the way, I became a part of those mysterious trips. I became the girl who I wondered about, who got to sit in the passenger seat of the Cadillac. I had dined, danced, and been dazzled by him. He had shown me a side to life I didn't know existed, and I craved it like a drug.

Now we are here. No business, no play—just sadness. Standing in front of a hospital and I do not want him to go. I want him. I need him. I love him. Yet I promised him, I would go, and a promise is a promise. So, I do the only thing that makes sense.

"Please kiss me," I ask, and I don't wait for him to respond before my lips are on his.

I kiss him. I kiss him like I will never kiss him or anyone ever again. It is sloppy, like me, but it is the realest thing about this moment and as I feel the taste of him and the warm embrace of his lips, I know that I can face anything that is coming when I walk through those doors.

"I'll see you soon," I tell him, as we release and I don't know if it's true, but I have to hope to heaven that it is, because I have only gotten a bite of "Mr. Camacho" and I want to experience all that is him.

As we get into her sparkling white Lexus my mother looks at me in a brutal coalescence of horror and disgust.

"You look horrible," she tells me. I haven't seen myself, haven't had the desire or thought to look in the mirror, but I know she is right.

"Yeah."

"They aren't quite ready for you yet," she begins and then makes an audible and dramatic cough. "Can you please have a mint or something?" She says shuffling through her purse until she finds a tub of peppermints and shakes them at me. I want to throw them out the window, but I take one as I roll my eyes and sigh.

"I need you to stop somewhere," I say, looking forward at nothing.

"Where?" she asks.

"I don't know, I don't care," I begin, but then I spot a drugstore across the way and point at it. "There's fine."

"For what?" She asks angrily.

"Cigarettes."

It's a partially true answer, but not my real reason. She drives. When we make it across the street, I barrel out of the car without saying a word. I have never been to this store, but I head from the parking lot to the liquor aisle as though it is second nature. I realize I am short on time and resources and will have to be convenient, so I quickly pick a 4-pack of individual small bottles of red wine and head to the checkout. I'm back to the car in minutes.

Before my mother can say a word, I crack the lid to the first miniature wine bottle and begin to down it.

The wine is cheap and tastes slightly of vinegar, but it does the job. I don't savor it, I devour it, and quickly open another after I am done with the first as my mother pulls into a secluded parking lot on the east side of the hospital.

"They are ready for you," she says.

That's great, I think, *but am I ready for them?* I have no idea what I am walking into. I down one more of the small bottles before we go in and finish half of a cigarette.

My mother and I enter a brightly lit lobby. I make no effort to greet the nurse at the front desk and sit down in one of the waiting chairs, exhausted. My mother returns with a clipboard and a pile of paperwork which evokes an audible groan from me.

"You can fill it out," I tell her with a wave of my hand.

A woman who looks nothing medical emerges from sliding glass doors. Her auburn hair is in a slick ponytail and she is in a well-tailored royal blue dress that is adorned with a white blazer. Her red lipstick accents the entire outfit and makes her look like she is more ready far more ready for a press conference than meeting the likes of me.

"Hannah?" She asks, extending her hand to me as she approaches. I take it.

"Yeah," is all I say, confused by the woman and who she is.

"I'll be taking you back," she tells me, "Doctor N. will be in soon to meet you, but for now we will start getting your intake done. You're our only patient on the floor right now."

For the entirety of my stay, I am the only patient in the detox ward. I am coming off of a cocktail of booze, benzos, and Suboxone, and the good doctor is frank with me from the start that this will be hell.

"Let's just get it over with," I tell him about my resolve to come off of everything at once, "Be done with it."

He tells me I will live, but that the third day will be the worst, and he is right. On Saturday, the day before Easter, I awake to my skin crawling. I feel like spiders are dancing beneath my skin and I think I see something, or someone move along the window, but I am not sure.

Mind over matter. It isn't real and this will be over. Only, it gets worse as the hours of the day go on.

I call my brother. Shadows are haunting my peripheral vision and I keep squeezing my eyes shut and opening them wide to try to get them to disappear to no avail.

"Sounds like delirium tremens," he says, a veteran of detoxing himself. "You need to tell the doctor."

But I don't, because I am okay. I have to be okay. I am just getting this under control.

A social worker who calls herself 'Bonnie' asks to meet with me to discuss my possible admission to rehab. Her voice is shrill, and she fumbles with the phone as she misdials the number twice. The admissions representative on the other line is asking me questions that I know should be simple, but I cannot answer them, and finally I announce:

"I cannot do this," and rise from my seat in a haste and retreat to my room and shut the door. The shadows are in front of me now, crawling up the wall, and cold sweat is pooling in the crevices of my collar bones.

Bonnie bursts into my room without knocking causing me to startle backwards onto my bed.

"Are you okay?" she asks.

"Yes, I just want to rest," I snap, and she looks at me with cold eyes but nods.

As she turns, she slams my door shut and the sound of it rings in my ears and sends a panic through my body. It reminds me of a gunshot, and I am unhinged as air becomes a luxury. No matter how hard I try to take it in, I feel like I cannot get enough oxygen.

I feel my heartbeat hard in my chest, and can feel it thumping in my hands, in my legs. I try to kill one of the creeping shadows with a nearby pen by flinging it at the wall with all my might and an involuntary scream leaves my mouth.

I am going to die today, I realize. My body is not supposed to be doing this.

I want my mom. I want my son. I want Henry. I am never going to see any of them again though, as I have the pressing obligation that time is running out and running out fast.

I retrieve the pen from the ground, scrounging for it on the linoleum floor as I try to only think about where my journal is. I have to write something down, because there is no way I am getting out of this room.

By some miracle I make it to my bed with both pen and paper and begin scrawling names in the margins: Hayden, Henry, Mom. I write them each a messy paragraph: *I love you, I'm sorry, please be okay*—in some fashion.

The shadows are gliding around the paper now and I scream at them—a loud shrill sound coming from my throat like vile poison.

In a few seconds the door to my room opens again and I cower beneath my blanket but drop it when I see Dr. N. somewhere between the dancing demons.

"I'm going to die," is all I say, as I feel a blood pressure cuff tightening around my bicep.

The numbers on the screen don't make sense, but I see the worry in his eyes reflect my own as he reads them.

"Ativan, stat!" he barks at a nurse.

I am shaking in his grasp.

"It's going to be okay," he tells me. "Hang on."

There is pressure in the IV that is lodged into the side of my wrist, and then I am swimming. I feel like I am drowning, as I begin to see flashes of white, like the bottom of that porcelain tub again, but my breathing becomes easier.

I make it through the night, and into the next day—Easter. I feel like I too have been resurrected as I am able to see the world without shadows and with a sobering clarity. The terror of the day before has, however, not worn off.

Henry is my only visit that day and the only one I want to see and for the first time I am able to agree with him, that I may have a problem.

DOSTOEVSKY DIDN'T PREPARE ME FOR THIS

April 25-May 17, 2019

Much to my expected rehab's chagrin, I have decided to return to my house before admittance to retrieve some belongings. I feel better than I did two days ago but I am still visibly shaking, and my head is clouded by large doses of sedatives to keep me from seizing or hallucinating.

As we approach the house, I try to hide my hands in the sleeves of the hoodie I have on. The tops of them are mottled in a hideous arrangement of blue and purple bruises from the multiple IVs I have been given over the past few days, and the coloring sticks out amongst the pale gray tone of my flesh.

"Oh my God," exclaims my mother, as we walk in and she examines the mess that is my living space.

There are piles of clothes everywhere and I know there is an assortment of empty liquor and wine bottles stashed all over the place.

"How do you find anything?" she asks in disgust.

I say nothing, scoffing in reply as I run to my room to stuff my bloodied bed sheets into the closet and begin collecting clothes, I see that look relatively clean. I haven't actually really lived out of here in quite some time, having spent most days either out of town or at Henry's as of late.

"We *have* to be there by two," my mother insists, and I pretend to care but really wonder what will happen if we aren't.

Residential rehab was not part of the deal when I first

arrived at Huntington Hospital. I was not inclined to do this, but I reluctantly agreed.

Our drive would take us all the way across Los Angeles to the coast, near Santa Monica. I sent my last few messages out to concerned friends, Henry, and a few family members. I also chatted back and forth with my brother; whose worry was apparent.

"You've gotten through the hardest part," the text read. *"I'm really proud of you for doing this."*

I wished I felt proud of me too, but more than anything I felt confused and still so sick, trying as hard as I could to focus on the words the social worker had told me:

"It's not forever," she had beamed, and it wasn't. It was 30 days, and while that seemed like a lot, I could do it.

When we arrive my mother chats with the director of the program as I take in my new living space. It looks nothing like I had expected, emanating nothing medical or hospital-like with its crystal fireplace, lofty staircase, and ultra-modern kitchen. What I don't see, is another soul in sight.

I watch with suspicion as my mother whispers to the woman who will be doing my intake and wonder what horrors she is already filling her head with.

"I'm not a child," I break in. "I would like to be involved in whatever my treatment looks like."

The modest-looking woman appears startled but then relaxes.

"Of course," she smiles. "Your mom and I were just discussing payment."

I shrug off the comment and take in more of my new living space. A smiling, but silent Hispanic woman takes my bags to my room as I gawk at the space around me. The house looks like something out of reality television, and I am in the center of it.

Eventually my mother leaves and I give her a farewell with a one-armed hug. I am cringing at the fact that the man who was once my boss and became my lover has talked my mother into putting me into rehab, but here I am.

A beaming girl with sea-blue eyes takes my vital signs and asks me a barrage of questions I am too tired to answer. I offer her one-word responses until I am finally allowed to leave, and chain smoke the carton of cigarettes I have brought.

I smoke cigarette after cigarette and can feel my throat becoming raw. In the midst of my pursuance of lung cancer, a giant beast of a boy walks out, teetering between his massive legs. He is wearing an incredible, oversized neon yellow hoodie sweatshirt that swallows his thin, lanky frame alive and patched blacked jeans. He motions at my carton.

"Can I have one?" he asks.

"Sure," I say, amused by the fact that we both look like hell. He reminds me of Big Bird from *Sesame Street*, if the giant puppet was completely strung out, and this guy very quickly tells me that he was.

"Smoking percs and snorting coke erryday—" he says with a laugh that should be trademarked. His name is Flynn and he flies, even in this sorry state.

We laugh about our sordid affair for a long while, and eventually go to bed, but our cigarette rendezvous become the highlight of my time at the luxury detox house—until the third day.

I'm sitting in the giant master bedroom that is all mine, flipping the channels on the television. It is my first day off of any sedatives and I will be doing a "test run" at the residential house in groups before being moved over there permanently.

I can't remember the last time I watched cable television, but land on a reality-TV dating show that looks mildly entertaining in passing before there is a knock at my door.

"Yes?"

The door opens. It's Tali, my interim counselor before I am moved to permanent residential housing.

"Hey Hannah," she is looking at the floor. "I need you to come downstairs for a phone call, it's your mom."

I say nothing as I rise. Something is wrong, no doubt. My blackout period of phone privileges is not over, and the look in Tali's eyes tells me all I need to know. Something has happened, and very likely, someone is dead. My first thought is that it is my grandfather. He has had an abundance of health problems—diabetes, multiple heart attacks, countless hospital stays—something must have taken him. I brace myself.

"Hey mom," I say, as Tali's work iPhone is already on speaker in the backyard.

"I'm so sorry Hannah," is how she starts the conversation.

I was right.

"What's wrong?" I ask.

"Carrie passed away this morning."

What? I feel like I've been hit. That was not the name I was expecting. And how? Carrie, my brother's wife. Carrie, who I just saw. Carrie, who sat with me in the hospital. How is she possibly dead? I feel tears stinging my eyes as I ask myself these questions in my head and finally am able to ask.

"How?"

"I'm still trying to get all the details," she begins, "but she drove the truck off an embankment, wasn't wearing a seatbelt and the car flipped onto her. They airlifted her into Anchorage but there was nothing they could do. Again, I'm sorry…"

Yeah, me too. I try to find my breath as I think of Zak and wonder if he is okay. This whole ordeal is so unfair—his life. Our tumultuous childhood, his PTSD from being sent into a war that he was too young to understand, the number of friends he has had killed or who have killed themselves, and now his wife—dead.

"I need to call my brother," I announce.

"You'll be able to tonight," Tali says, with a half-smile. I can tell she has no idea what to do. "And look, if you don't want to go over to residential today and just want to rest…"

"No—" I break in immediately, "I do. I'll go."

I get up to go ready myself because that is what Zak would do. Not stop, and if I stop now, I may start thinking.

There is too much echoing silence as I brush my hair and put on a light coat of makeup and my thoughts begin to get loud.

Carrie was there, after that horrible morning. After all of that water, all of that blood, after the gunshot, after I seized—in the ambulance, holding my hand, with Zak trailing behind us in his trooper car.

What was it she was saying to the paramedic? I know it, I know it very well, I just don't want to say it or think of it because it is so morbid and feels so wrong. I can hear their conversation like it was happening right in front of me again though, as it was the only noise, I focused on in that ambulance ride. The massive vehicle flopped and bumped along the unpaved Alaskan backroads and I shook with panic and fear from all that had just happened.

Don't have a panic attack and *don't have another seizure* were my two rules for myself during that ride. To do that, I focused on nothing but the sound of Carrie and the paramedic's voices and what they were saying.

Carrie was telling him about her own experience being an EMT and paramedic in Denver before coming up to Alaska with my brother.

A bump and I feel the belts on the gurney dig into my flesh.

"Ouch," she says, laughing, "You good sweetie?"

I let out a weak nod and she continues talking to the paramedic.

"You know, I never used to wear my seatbelt on transports, my husband couldn't stand it!" she tells him, "but it made it so much harder to work on the patient."

There it is. Chekhov's gun...or belt in this case.

It's the first thing I think of in this moment, as I often live in literary references. One of my "goals for treatment" that I have written down is to start reading again. I can't remember the last time I finished a book. I seem to always be buying them, starting them, and then abandoning them to my endless shelves. The thought makes me sad. All I used to do was read.

My childhood memory is spotty at best, but I remember that. Reading faster and more eagerly than any of the children in my class, writing papers that always brought smirks to my English teachers' faces, midday trips to the public library to look at forbidden mainstream books that weren't in my father's approved list of C.S. Lewis. This love had followed me, and I had achieved a degree in English Literature from a good university, gushing over my 20th century Lost Generation heroes and my love for Russian greats like Dostoevsky and Pushkin. I had loved *Crime and Punishment* so much I had read it almost ten times and wrote a thesis about it. Do you see me now Rodion Raskolnikov?

"Pain and suffering are always inevitable for a large intelligence and a deep heart."—I can see the line, circled in messy black pen, in the big brick-sized book in front of me now.

Is that the root of all my problems? Probably not. My brain feels broken, as I am having trouble remembering even small things right now and my heart feels stoic and on the verge of shattering. The news of Carrie's demise isn't helping.

Later that night I do talk to Zak and he tells me about what is being dubbed as a "tragic accident" through broken sobs. She was thirty seconds from the house, and from just being there, I know exactly where. He tells me in goring detail about how the truck caved her skull in and half of her face being ripped off. The description makes me nauseous and uncomfortable, but I say nothing, only listening, as I know this is what he needs.

"Please just focus on yourself, and get better, because I am going to need you," he tells me.

"I will," I tell him, and I mean it, though I don't know what *getting better* means. I would be there for him no matter what. Zak and I have always been the distinct black sheep of the family, and this has built a bond for us stronger than blood. I would do anything for him.

"I love you, and again, I'm so sorry."

It feels like a stupid thing to say, a cliché and pathetic thing to say, but what is there to say? His wife is dead. Nothing is going to fix that. Especially not me, over 3,000 miles away and locked in a treatment center.

I take in small morsels of the rich food prepared by the treatment center's private chef that night amongst my new company: nine men, most of whom are really still boys, an older woman who is about to leave, and a girl, my age, who has no interest in speaking to anyone, but her eyes seethe with anger. All but the latter hear of my dilemma and shower me with support that makes me uncomfortable, but I smile at their kind comments.

That night I do not find sleep, and for the rest of my time at rehab, I become very reacquainted with my long-lost insomnia. Life was easier when I could drown myself to sleep with pills and/or booze, but here I was, stuck with my head.

When I did get sleep, it was like immediately being plunged into a lake and I would very quickly awake and come up for air. So instead of pursuing rest, I read. I read and read and read into the early hours of dawn until my eyes hurt and the books, I finish become a neat, tall stack as I leave—two days before my planned discharge, on a Friday.

Alex greets me, standing cool in his leather work boots leaning against his Prius as I throw my things into his car. Within two hours I have a glass of wine in my hand, on his dime.

After a glass of wine and two whiskeys, he is too drunk to drive and the thought of getting behind the wheel of a car makes me freeze in place. We both toddle to the beach and sit in the sand. I let it sift through my fingers as I avoid gazing into the water and look at him.

He looks like shit. His thick brown hair needs a good cut and a wash, he is at least fifteen pounds underweight, and the skin beneath his eyes sinks in like caverns. Yet he stares at me with his massive, perpetually sad brown eyes and I see his lip quiver. Never the emotional type, never with anyone but me.

"I still love you; you know."

And I do know, I know very well. It's why I called him, because I knew he would drive across Los Angeles in rush hour at a beckon call to get me.

"Is it worth it?" he asks me.

"Is what worth it?"

"Him." Henry. "That piece of shit."

That piece of shit. I've heard that one before.

It was the middle of night in early January. I was sleeping in my son's room, despite him being gone at his dad's house, but Alex and I were nothing more than roommates now. We had been for a time, our relationship long ended and our shared living space a matter of convenience.

Five years of being together had made him keen to chatting with me though, especially in the middle of the night when he couldn't sleep and was drinking.

That night I was startled from sleep with a roaring "WHAT THE FUCK?!" and the sound of something slamming against the wall. As I stumbled from my daze, I clambered to see what it was. My phone. The name on the screen —Henry.

The message spoke for itself.

"How long have you been fucking that piece of shit?" he had screamed at me.

Now here we were, months later.

"He's a good guy," I protest, staring at the sand.

"He is your boss, and he is...how old again? 35...45? Fuck, I don't care. I don't even know who you are anymore."

"39," I say.

"Yeah, that's fucking gross."

I ignore the comment. I've heard it all before.

"You know, sometimes I just want to fucking kill him."

Christ, he is drunk. I wonder if he had something before he got here. Probably.

"Alex—" I start, but he interrupts me.

"No, I'm serious. That piece of shit..." there it is again, "ruined my family. Hayden is God-knows-where and you're fucking your boss who is twice your age."

"A technicality," I say, and laugh.

"Do you love him?"

Of course I do, but I don't say that, because I can feel the hurt that is coursing through Alex.

"Come on," I command, getting up and offering him my hand. "It's getting cold and I think it's time for another drink."

For all the things we have fought over, he has never argued with me on that front.

I scrutinize him as we walk to the nearest bar. I was going to be this man's bride and now we are just two broken souls, walking down a boulevard in Santa Monica, looking for the next escape. Without thinking, I seize his arm and turn him towards me and hug him.

Despite his skeleton-like frame, I had forgotten how small I was next to him as my head hits his sternum and he lets out a sigh.

"It's going to be okay," I whisper, but as I release him and he scrunches his face and his brown eyes screech distrust, I know he doesn't believe me. I don't believe me either.

DEAD MEANS DEAD

May 19, 2019

It's a beautiful Spring morning and my head is slightly throbbing from the copious amounts of wine I have consumed over the past few days, but I am okay. Just hungover, not drunk and not drinking. It's time to get back to real life.

Henry is awake and about. It's Monday, but I know I won't be going back to work, not yet. In fact, the topic hasn't really come up.

In my absence, he has moved the giant California King sized bed from the center of the room to the back wall and I haven't decided if I like the change. What I am grateful for though, is that I am back. I haven't braced the disaster of my own home yet, the place I pay rent for, but in my heart, this feels like home to me.

"Want some coffee?" he asks me, and I nod. It will likely settle my headache and get me back on the path I need to be on for the coming week.

The past 30 days gave me a reset, which was all I really needed. Things had gotten out of control, and I had regained that control, and was planning to execute it in every aspect of my life.

Henry is soon back with the coffee and sets it on the windowsill. The steam rising from it tells me it is still too hot to drink. I try to settle into the mess of sheets on the bed and am grateful for the fact that I don't have to be anywhere or do anything on a Monday morning, but I am suddenly startled by the sound of my phone ringing.

It is still foreign to me that I have a phone again after being without one for 30 days. In a way, this is one of the things I appreciate most about my time from rehab as I have started to be more present in social situations without the escape of a handheld screen. Nonetheless, I follow the noise to the other room and glance at the glowing screen.

Mom.

I think of the time. I had expected she would check in with me at some point today, but it is before 9:00. I answer.

"Hello?"

"Hi..." She begins. Something is wrong.

"Hey is everything okay?"

"No, no it isn't—" a long pause. The words that follow feel like a massive dagger going through my chest. I feel every muscle in my body tense as if I have braced for an impact too late. The words do not make sense, they can't, but as soon as she says them, I know, without a shred of doubt in my mind that they are true.

I drop the phone and as it clatters to the floor, my entire body crumbles into Henry and from my mouth comes a sound —a scream, a cry, a wailing I did not know I was capable of making. Tears are spilling like rivers from my eyes and they feel like blood.

I grab onto Henry's shirt, trying to grasp him for any sort of support, because I can barely stand.

His eyes are frantic as he asks me: "What! What! What is it?!"

I don't know how, I do not know why, I do not know where, but I know one thing and it becomes an anthem. It becomes my truth. Because when I asked my mother if everything was okay, little did I know that nothing would be okay for a very long time after she gave me the fatal response.

"My brother is dead!" I shriek.

I say it again.

And again.

And again.

And again.

And I don't know how many times I say it, but I shake, and I sob and something in my mind shuts off because my brain cannot make sense of what is happening.

In between harsh realizations I try and deduce what is going on. *Zak cannot be dead*, I think. *Carrie is dead. Carrie just died.* But then again, I didn't understand how Carrie could be dead either. How were they both dead? And why, why, why, why was I alive?

I am no longer at the house. My mind sees flashes of darkness, of a lake like a mirror, of blood, of Carrie's caved in skull, of my brother's cold, dead body. This is somebody's fault. Things like this do not just happen.

My heart is racing. My head is pounding. *Kill it*, a voice inside of me says, *fucking kill it*. And I have to, but how?

At some point my mother arrives and Henry gives us the room. In the midst of my madness I have called my father. I was the one to tell him his son is dead. I feel nothing about this. In fact, I blame him.

My mother just tells me, "I'm sorry."

I want to spit on her. Her apology and her sympathy don't mean shit.

Then I spot it, right through the glass in the cabinet in my peripheral. *Vodka.* Maybe there is a God.

As my mother keeps talking and trying to console me, I

yank the door to the cabinet open and open the vodka bottle and have it to my mouth in a matter of seconds.

My mother looks at me in a mixture of disgust and horror.

"Hannah—"

"DO NOT fucking tell me what to do right now," I command her.

She says nothing more about the matter.

"You can leave," I tell her, retreating with my liquor to the back room of the house. I slosh the clear liquid around in its glass container. It isn't much and it won't be enough, but it is a start.

I don't want her; I don't want her sympathy. I don't want anyone or anything. I hate God, or the universe, or whatever the fuck is playing this celestial joke on me. There were so many awful people in the world, I knew a few. Why couldn't one of them die? No, of course, one of the few people I believe in and who believed in me, who has seen me through hell, is going to be in the ground.

As I tell God He can eat shit and strike me down with lightning for all I care, I realize with a great terror that Henry is probably next with the way things are going. I drink.

My head is beginning to spin, but I am only just starting. I do not want to be anything close to awake or feeling like I am alive right now.

Henry knocks on the doorframe.

"Hey," he says, seeing the vodka. I immediately know he is going to try and take it away and clutch it with all of my strength and scream at him.

"MY FUCKING BROTHER IS DEAD!" It's true after all. And he's going to be dead too. Everyone is going to die. I think of my brother's life, his shit, tragic life and how the last good thing he did was save my worthless one before his wife died.

Everyone is going to die. I may as well die first, and as I take feverish sips of vodka, this seems like a good way to do it.

Red may mean dead, but so do a lot of other things I am starting to realize. A bad turn, too many pills, a bottle, a knife, cruelty, or just plain stupidity—or these things can mean nothing at all. Anything can be a lethal weapon, including words, it just depends what you do with them.

PART II
THE BREAKDOWN

POST-TRAUMATIC STRESS DISASTER

July 1, 2019

Nothing inside of me feels right—but I am home, or what I am calling home for now. Earlier today I left treatment in a rush, gathering my things in a hurry and leaving without a trace in under ten minutes. Being in Orange County again was part of what was contributing to my deteriorating mental state, and I had made a firm resolution not to go back as Henry and I sat in silence racing up the freeway towards Pomona.

The arrival home isn't a happy one. As he opens the door, I see his beloved boxer dog, Cooper, lying on the floor struggling for air and unable to move. Henry rushes to situate his head back onto a dog bed and then leaves the room in an anguish. I kneel next to Cooper and stroke his brittle coat and let out a pained sigh. I've worked with enough animals to know he won't make it much longer, maybe not even another day, but I cannot tell Henry this.

A wave of paranoia washes over me and I feel the sudden compulsion to check outside the door. I should feel safe, but I don't. It's the sudden inkling that something terrible is about to happen, and as I glance back at Cooper I realize—it is.

Later that night, Henry has situated Cooper on a couch adjacent to us; we watch him carefully as he goes in and out of sleep.

Henry lets out a sigh, "Can you go to the store? I don't want to leave him alone."

I hesitate but nod. I haven't been out on my own in weeks. I feel like I am starting to forget how to function.

He gives me a list of very simple things he needs—Q-tips, deodorant, water bottles, and a bag of chips. He tells me to get whatever I need as he hands me a credit card.

"I'll be back," I promise, as I head outside to wait for the ride he has arranged for me.

The argument of me getting my car back has been squashed. Prior to it being repaired and detailed, it looked like I had repeatedly banged it into a wall from repeated collisions while I was drinking. The inside made it look as though I had simply used the vehicle as wastebin between the stashes of wine and whiskey bottles and forgotten trash I had left behind. My loved ones hardly trusted me to take a walk, I was a long way from operating a two-ton machine.

Yet here was Henry, on my first night back—allowing me this risk of freedom. I knew in my mind it was only the situation that allowed it, and the shard of conscience I have is screaming at me not to take advantage of it.

I make it to the store and go straight to the aisles where the items he requested will be, grabbing a few toiletries for myself. When I have everything, I know I should head to the checkout, but I don't. I go to the place where I promised myself I wouldn't, to the far right of the store—the liquor aisle. I don't go to the spirits, but instead to the wines, contemplating the small, personal-size boxed varieties. I could probably fit two, maybe three inside of my purse.

I stare at the little purple box. It stares at me. I want it. I want it. I want it. But something happens—I see Cooper, I think of his ribs rising and falling under my hands earlier that day, and I think of Henry. He needs me right now, and in some strange evocation, I curse the box.

I return home and give Henry the things he asks for and at some point, I decide to go sleep.

It's late and pitch black when I am awoken by the sound of ragged sobbing. I feel immediately awake, and I know what has happened, but Henry confirms it with his words.

"He's g-gone," he weeps, falling into my arms and I hold him as his cries break my heart into a million pieces.

I feel his body heave and try to rock him and infuse any semblance of calm I can into him, because there is nothing to say. All I want to do is make it better, to not see him in pain, but I know there is nothing I can do.

Then it comes to me, and I think of the decision I made hours before—and I am so grateful I did not drink, that I did not make this moment infinitely worse for him, that he is not alone.

But then another, much darker realization hits me. I think of Carrie, I think of Zak—both dead, both gone, and I am still convinced of my role in this somehow. And now, on my first night back here, Cooper.

Henry rises in the early hours of the morning to take Cooper's body to be cremated and I am left alone in the quiet solitude of the house. I have had too much time to think about all that has happened over the last month and a half and have skimmed the surface of things I never wanted to touch. I tried to run from it, but instead I feel like I have a gaping wound that needs mending, but I know not how to salve it.

I feel the sudden urge to check the window again, make sure nothing is there, and nothing is. The street is quiet, the world is quiet, but my head is not.

I am not good at honesty, not with others and not with myself, and I think that this is a learned habit. Yet sitting here, again, at the end of a bout of treatment, with another death at hand, and with only my own mind, I cannot help but think of the truth.

The truth that my dear brother went to his grave with and saved me the shame from and now that piece of human garbage walks the planet free as a bird. The truth of April 2nd.

I got to Anchorage in the dead of night and the Man with the Red Hair was waiting for me at the baggage claim. Icicle eyes to match his icicle soul. As we drove through out of the dump that is Alaska's largest city, my only thought was of doom. That ominous feeling of "Oh God I am at the end of the world and I am stuck here." And all I wanted was Henry and home.

We stopped at a Taco Bell. I wasn't hungry. But what I did want was a soda to pour my vodka into because I knew I was, in a word—

fucked. I had drunkenly flown myself 3,000 miles away from home and was with a man who I knew had the potential to be dangerous.

He told me he would take me to my brother's, but I knew the second I saw him that would not or never be happening. My brother didn't even know I was here.

Two years prior: we were all at the cabin. It was the end of September and it was so clear and beautiful. I was screaming at Zak when I opened the trunk to his truck and piles of vodka bottles started spilling out. He lit a cigarette and left me with his wife, my manic fiancée, and two strangers.

"Seems like you need a break," one of the strangers said to

me. He was rugged with red hair and blue eyes. "Want to actually see Alaska?"

I cocked my head. This was Alaska, as Alaska as Alaska could be. This man had a porcupine stuck to a tree with an axe at the front of his property. We surely were not in California anymore.

"Come hop on the motorcycle with me." He said, "We are gonna barbeque tonight and I gotta get some stuff, come with me."

I looked at my fiancée, who was taking silent sips of Jim Bean and puffs from his own cigarette, asking for permission. He was oblivious, so I finally asked.

"Can I go?" I asked.

"I don't know how I feel about you on a motorcycle," he said, "but go for it."

So, I did and as I was on the back of that motorcycle, I saw the speed needle continue to go right until it flirted with 120. I clung to the back of this stranger's back, as I was sure I was going to die, but I had this overwhelming feeling of unconcern. I felt like a bird.

When he stopped, it was by a creek. We walked to the corner of it, and with no hesitation, I rolled up my jeans, took off my boots, and ran into it. Little fish danced around my feet and I laughed.

"You are so beautiful," he told me, "The most beautiful thing I have ever seen. He doesn't deserve you."

I said nothing, but then he asked me, "What do you want? Out of life?"

"Family." Was what I said, without hesitation, "And freedom."

And in that moment, I felt like I had the latter.

He raped me on the bank of the same creek two years later and killed the baby I didn't know I had inside of me in the wave of violence of that April night.

That was really the first death in this string of everything around me dropping dead. It seemed the grim reaper was leaving a trail around anything I touched.

A few days after Cooper's death we are at what used to be our weekly clubbing spot in Downtown Pomona. Henry's friend from his days as a DJ is playing and something in me is eager to be back on the dancefloor. It was like we never left the scene, as we follow our usual routine—heading to a pub first to order two old fashioneds with our signature bourbon. This drink tastes like us, I think, as I let the whiskey warm me while Henry brushes my leg with a tender hand. It makes me feel better that I am not the only one who tries to numb my pain.

The night goes on and goes off, as we both go home in a blacked-out stupor. The difference is, it ends there for Henry. For me, it ends a few days later, in the psych ward.

NOT YOUR GOLDEN GIRL

July 10-13, 2019

They tell me I am in Pasadena and the sky is clear here. I wonder how the weather is in San Francisco, as I think of how incredible the Golden Gate Bridge can look on a clear day. That's where I am supposed to be. In some distorted fantasy, I had pictured Henry taking me back to the place where he had lived for so many years and getting down on one knee in Golden Gate Park and asking me to be his wife.

That was not reality though, and with the way things were going, it was not close to ever going to be. My reality was that on the night before we were supposed to go to the Bay, I had downed an ungodly amount of vodka and was brought back to the house at two in the morning by the police. In the morning, I drank down an entire bottle of Angostura bitters like they were an antidote for a poison coursing through my veins and then…and then…I look at the gaping gashes on my left wrist and cringe.

I arrived here late in the night and it has been two days. I am still confused as to what is going on and where I am. This is supposed to be a mental hospital, but the building I am in looks more like a cramped cabin. It holds six people, one of which is me, the only female.

One of the men is bearded and has been huddled in the corner of the main front room all morning, pulling at his facial hair and talking to himself. Two of the others I have seen looked at me as if I am choice meat, ready to be devoured and they frighten me. Another looks to be about my age and has a wolfish face and smirks at absolutely nothing in the distance, as if he is concocting some sort of plan. Then there is a new one who is old and haggard and is annihilating the sorry excuse for scrambled eggs that has been served for breakfast. The yellow juice and globs of grease that coagulate around the eggs is now dripping down this pathetic man's face, and the sight makes me want to vomit, but also gives me an idea. I check to make sure the staff isn't looking.

"Want mine?" I ask very eagerly, because I have no desire to eat anything, let alone this.

"GOD BLESS YOU!" He roars, "I WILL ASK HIM TO BLESS YOU."

I roll my eyes and quickly spoon my eggs onto the man's plate as the wolfish boy chuckles.

"I TALK TO GOD," the egg man asserts, "I'm talking to him right now. Do you want to ask him anything?"

"No," is all I say. Now the wolfish boy is choking on his laughter.

"Say," the man says, scarfing my serving of eggs into his mouth, "You really look like Audrey Hepburn. Would you dance for me?"

I look at him with utter disgust and then look at the clock, it's time for my Ativan and I thank God for that. I throw away my plate and head to the nurse's station, get my drugs, and retreat to my room as I let the mild feeling of oblivion and escape wash over me.

As the lightness in my head becomes more intense, I examine my right foot. There is a massive gash running across it and it looks like it is going to get infected, but I don't care. In my Ativan-induced stupor the day prior I had fallen and caught my flesh on a bolt sticking from the wall. I didn't feel much from it, but the caked blood on my sheets makes it clear that it was a messy ordeal. I want out of here.

A knock on the door and the staff member of my nightmares makes himself welcome. I am not sure what he is supposed to be, but I hate him.

His name is Chris. Beneath his scrubs I can see his fleshy, overweight body. His messy dark hair looks unwashed and comes down like a mop around his eyes but doesn't hide the smile he has as he shuts the door behind him.

"How are you feeling?" He asks.

"Fine," I whisper.

"Who was that guy yesterday?" He asks, referring to the visit I got from Henry. "That your boyfriend or something?"

I nod.

"He must think he struck gold with a pretty thing like you," he coos. "Surprised he hasn't knocked you up yet."

Chris gets close to me and suddenly I can smell him. He reeks of fast food and his breath smells stale has he blows hot air onto me.

"I bet I could knock you up in one try," he laughs and strokes my hair, then grabs the back of my neck.

I can feel the tears forming in my eyes as I shut them as hard as I can. I want to hit him. I want to scream, but I want to get out of here. The smell of Chris grows weaker and I feel his grip loosen. I open my eyes and a stream of tears falls.

"You know most of them are in here for homicidal ideation," he giggles, "They probably all want to fuck you, but at least half of them want to kill you then fuck you."

My tears keep falling and I say nothing.

"You know I wouldn't let anyone hurt you though, right?"

"Go. Away." I finally mutter.

He lets out a scoff and I see him relishing in my tears.

"I'll see you in a bit," he promises, and I know he means it and I know I need to get on the phone and that I need to figure out how I am going to get out of here.

In the meantime, I sleep. When I wake up it is still light outside, but all is silent, and I ruminate on how much I hate myself as I stare at the white ceiling. I want more Ativan, but I know it isn't time yet and I think of what to do. I sit for a long time and wrap myself in the blood-caked, sweat-stained sheets that the staff have yet to change out for me, and I doubt that they will.

Another knock at the door. *Chris again*, I think, and I feel the bile in my stomach rise. I want to shout, "go away" or "fuck off", but instead I just wrap myself further in the sheets, as though they will protect me.

The door doesn't open and there is another knock. Now I am both curious and irritated.

I let out a croaky, "Wha-at?" as I lift my head slightly and the door opens slowly.

It isn't Chris. It's the egg-prophet man and he is wearing a gaping smile. It shows off blackened, rotting teeth and spaces with no teeth at all. His presence confuses me, and he is walking towards me, but before I can react or ask questions, he pulls his right hand from behind his back and throws a rag straight at my face and retreats from my room in a hurry.

I immediately feel something dripping down my skin from where the cloth hit and shut my mouth so whatever it is doesn't enter. Feeling my face, the substance sticks to my fingers and creates a film on my hand. I open my eyes and right away, I know what it is and I want to scream.

Before a shriek can leave my mouth, Chris and a nurse are in my room and are staring at me and the mess across my face.

"Did Lloyd just come in here?!" Chris shouts.

I nod, gritting my teeth. So, Lloyd is his name. Lloyd, the man who likes eggs. Lloyd, the man who asked me to dance. Lloyd, the man who talks to God.

"What. The. Fuck. Is. That?" Chris asks, pointing at the rag and then my face.

I can't even say it out loud and I don't have to, because before I can answer the question Lloyd is running down the hallway screaming with his pants down.

"That dumb whore wouldn't dance for me!" is all I hear.

Chris and the nurse leave me and the mess that is on my face and I begin to hear sounds of crashing outside. I take my bloody sheet and hide behind the little oaken closet that is in my room, and for the first time in months, maybe in years. I begin to actually pray.

"Please God," is all I say, "Please help me," is the only prayer I know as I try to viciously wipe some madman's semen off my face and pray with all of my heart that he doesn't break into my room and kill me. And he doesn't, and eventually Chris returns.

"Lloyd is taken care of. Come on," Chris commands me, "We've got to get you cleaned up. God only knows what kind of diseases that fucking sick bastard has."

Right. I think, shaking as I get up from behind the closet. Because the truth is, Lloyd is just one kind of sick bastard, and at least he has madness as an excuse. Chris is just a pervert who thinks he has come to my rescue.

He delivers me to a female nurse who strips me down and shows me an industrial size bottle of some sort of wash.

"This will disinfect your skin," she tells me, as she lightly pushes me into the shower and pours the mixture over my hair. "Oh, close your eyes," she says, as the mixture drips down from my scalp to my face, and all over my body.

I am glad I thought of that myself because whatever this is burns like hell. I feel the slimy soap stinging at my skin, and in a way I am grateful, as I feel like it is burning Lloyd away, but as I touch my face I can feel little bumps already starting to form from where the disinfectant has touched me. But I let it burn, and I let the water cleanse me, and when I exit the shower, I am given more Ativan and I slip back into oblivion.

I am released the next day.

When my mother arrives and we leave the hospital and into her white Lexus, she remarks that "you really need a shower."

All I do is nod, but I want to tell her that I am sure I do, as my foot is now completely infected, I've been sleeping in disgusting, dirty sheets, and other than my disinfectant shower, I have not bathed much, but I keep my mouth shut.

"I need a cigarette," I say. "Now."

She puts up a protest, as I imagined she would, but eventually I get my wish and it tastes like heaven. As I take puffs of the stale smoke, it hits me that it is almost my birthday and Henry will be back soon and I need to make things right. More than anything, I can never ever go back to a place like that again. That starts with a change.

As I get back into the car, my mother remarks that I smell even worse now, and I ignore her sentiment completely.

"I need you to stop at the beauty supply store," I tell her.

"What?!" she remarks, shocked.

"Please, it's important."

"For what?"

"Bleach. I want to dye my hair blonde again," I say, examining the mousy brown it is in the reflection of her side mirrors.

My hair has been brunette for almost two years now, but I decide that if it is for even one more day, I will surely want to cut it all off because I want to look nothing like Audrey Hepburn, or whatever Lloyd's version of her is. Think I'll be more of a Marilyn.

SUMMERTIME SELF-LOATHING IN SIN CITY

July 21-23, 2019

I have made it through another birthday and while that in itself is shocking, I am more appalled that I didn't cry through it. I had an ocean view from a hotel, the man of my dreams, a three-course dinner planned for me, handpicked gifts, and love. In the days prior I had graced the walls of a mental institution. *They had not graced me*, I think, still itching at my peeling skin.

"We need to go to Vegas this weekend," Henry tells, not asks me, adding, "I have a doctor out there I have to meet with for business."

I fumble through the mess of mounds of psychiatric medications I have been prescribed in addition to Antabuse—a drug that allegedly will make me violently sick if I drink on it. I read stories about people turning tomato red, having soaring blood pressure, and not being able to breathe after trying to drink on the drug, and decide against it.

Las Vegas—sober. I haven't done that since I was ten, but it looks like that's in my cards.

"Sounds great," I say, and I am quickly arranging a therapy appointment to go to before we leave.

My last treatment center had been dull, at best, but it had provided me with a therapist who I liked and trusted, which is far and few between. I text Andre and set an appointment for the next day.

I wait for him in a medical building, outside of what is presumably, the office of his private practice. The air conditioning is either off or broken and the air in the building is stifling.

I look down at the pile of bags I have with me—my clothes, birthday gifts, books. I will be seeing my mother after this visit and choke on the expectations of that and the fact that if it gets bad enough, I cannot have a drink. I stopped taking the Antabuse two days ago, but from my reading it can last in one's system up to fourteen days. I know they will expect to watch me take it, but I am not new to hiding medication in my cheeks or dropping a pill in my sleeve before making it look like I have popped it in my mouth.

My thoughts are interrupted by the arrival of Andre. He looks cool and calm as usual, in designer sunglasses, a casual but bright button up shirt, slacks, and leather shoes. As he removes his glasses, I see the shock in his eyes as he takes in my now-blonde hair and the girlish blue dress I am wearing.

"Quite the makeover," he says. "I want to hear all about it."

He laughs and opens the door to his office, which I am grateful for, as I feel the blast of air conditioning as I walk through the doorframe.

It is quite the makeover. He is used to seeing me in all black, perhaps with a pop of burgundy if I was feeling colorful, and my hair brown and straight, covering sections of my eyes. I neglect to tell him about Lloyd during the session and I don't have to. There is enough to talk about. I tell him about my birthday.

"You stayed by the ocean!" he beams. "That's huge. Do you realize that? You couldn't even be around water before."

I remember all too well. The treatment center where we had met had been next to a bay, and I had been avoiding nature walks around it like the plague. During one of my few outings I took by myself during that time, I had gone down to Corona del Mar and tried to brace the beach on my own.

My vision got lost in the vastness of the ocean and I forgot where I was. I was no longer on the coast of California. I was in Alaska, on Lake Lucille, where the Man with the Red Hair had taken me after the creek. Where Zak had found me—bloodied, broken, naked, and shaking—dying.

Back in California, staring at the ocean, I felt like I was going to die again, until someone tapped me and asked if I was okay, seeing me hyperventilating and possessed by the water.

"No!" I wanted to shout, but instead I turned my vision to the jetty.

There was not a jetty on Lake Lucille, nothing like it, so I couldn't be there, but the panic had set in, so I said "yes, thank you," and turned to my phone as I ran from the ocean. Andre picked up after two rings and I told him of my dilemma, and he talked me into an Uber and to a local bookstore—and I lived.

Most people are dazzled by the ocean, especially the vast Pacific I grew up next to and still live near. Now it has become a tool of exposure therapy for me.

"I suppose it's an accomplishment," I finally produce, because in actuality I feel pathetic.

"How are your flashbacks?" he asks me, and I stare at nothing, fingering my still gaping wrist.

"Not good," is all I say, even though I know he wants more than that.

He doesn't ask for it though. He knows what I mean. This man has had to escort me through busy rooms to avoid panic attacks, sit with me in the sun through crying spells, have late night therapy sessions with me during my long nights of sleeplessness, and bring me out of the fearsome state I become lost to when I think back. He doesn't get paid enough for this.

I don't want to talk about my flashbacks or about my most recent ordeal at the mental hospital now, so I focus on my most pressing predicament—my brother's memorial service next week. I will be going, and I know I will be on display. The broken sister. My whole family will be there. My father will be there. *My father…*

I want Henry there with me. I need him there with me. I need something to hold onto as I walk into this living hell that cements the fact that my brother is gone and gone for good.

"Under no circumstances will he be there," my father instructed me. "This isn't about you."

No, it isn't. It isn't about Zak either. It's about him and his show for family, friends, and the do-gooders of Orange County who want to pay their respects to the man they didn't know. I just want to feel safe, but what Ron Cloe says goes.

"That's ridiculous," Andre tells me, when I share my father's sentiments with him. I know it is, half of my family agrees as well. Henry has been my rock, but he does not fit into my father's perfect picture, and that is more problematic than ever at this moment as I know he is trying to keep control over a situation where he has completely lost it.

I remind myself that I was the one, in my fury, who told him his son was dead, and stuff my resentment deep within me.

The session ends and I schedule another one, as well as an appointment with the psychiatrist he works with. I'll be seeing him soon, but first I am going to Vegas, and far, far away from here.

In two days, we are gone, and this time I am awake and somewhat alive, as I take sips of iced coffee as we melt into the lights of the Las Vegas Strip. As we emerge from the car in front of Caesar's Palace, I take in the throngs of people and wonder if I look insane.

Probably not. I am wearing a fitted, tie-dye blue dress I just bought that hugs my body well and strappy sandals that are perfect for the Vegas summer heat. I look the part; my head says otherwise.

Unlike our last trip, we do not stop at the bar upon our arrival. I am dying for a Jack and Coke in the middle of the casino—to be like every other sorry, sad, lost soul here, but I can't.

Fucking Antabuse, I think and curse my predicament. Maybe I'll take up a gambling addiction instead, because right now, I need something, anything, to get me out of my head and out of the noise of the people.

Henry leads me to the room which is on a redesigned tower of the hotel. The rooms are inspired by Japanese culture, and I silently appreciate the effort put in by the interior designers as I look at the low platform bed and paintings of cherry blossoms above the headboard.

Our room has a spectacular view, and I look at the postcard picture of the Las Vegas Strip right in front of my eyes. The window does not open, and it is clear why. I am sure it only took one bad drunken night for them to implement that feature. I wonder if the builders took into account girls who want to throw themselves from windows sober when they designed the rooms. Probably not.

Henry is ironing a shirt and I know that means I should also begin to ready myself for going out. I pick an orange dress that hugs my breasts and hips and would be hardly appropriate anywhere else. As I slip into it, I think of how much I hate the color orange. I feel like a piece of fruit peeled open with far too much skin showing for my liking. I prefer clothes that let me hide, and I am on display.

But as I walk out of the bathroom Henry emits a "wowza" as he eats me up with his eyes, and it has produced the effect I hoped for.

He likes me in colors, likes me looking like a woman—not like a gothic cretin who is being eaten alive by oversized sweaters.

I smile but feel immensely uncomfortable in the ensemble, but it is too late to change, and we go.

I have always loved Las Vegas, but for the first time, I am wondering if that was really love or just copious amounts of booze and cocaine.

Panic courses through my veins as I take in the masses of people in every direction I look. I search their faces, waiting to see one of my demons staring back at me, ready to kill me.

Henry grabs my hand several times throughout the night and I know he can feel my energy, my fear and my longing for oblivion. He can't give me a drink, so he tries the next best thing, as he takes me to a posh restaurant amongst the designer shops of Caesar's Palace.

"Look," he says, pointing at the menu. "They have your favorite."

Grilled cheese and tomato soup. It has been and still is one of my favorite combinations of food, and as I stare at the elaborate cocktails on the menu that I can't have, I hope that naïve nostalgia may salve my discomfort and discontent with life for a few minutes.

After dinner we emerge to the front of the hotel and sit on a platform where we share a cigarette and watch the tourists come to and from the entrance.

I think of our last trip here. Of us emerging, drunken and giggling from a Gwen Stefani concert, living and breathing Las Vegas and each other—with not a care in the world. Our throats were raw from screaming *No Doubt* songs at each other, both of our heads were spinning with drink, and nothing in the world mattered. No one had died yet; I was broken already but didn't feel a crack that night. The world was ours, and now we were at its mercy.

Henry makes quips about the characters who walk past us —a lady in a chiffon that looks like it was pulled off the back of an ostrich, an elderly, well-dressed man, with two 20-something blondes on each side of him, a couple fighting in a drunken rage.

He sees the people, but all I can see right now is him, and for a moment, my heart and my mind feel okay. Then I see it— a man in a Marine Corps T-shirt with a beer in hand, minding his own business. I say nothing, but my head is again flooded with the fact of what the upcoming week brings.

Carrie is dead. Zak is dead. I should be dead, but I am in Las Vegas, and I know that the night is winding down for the city that never sleeps, but is just starting for me—as the dead of night seems to be the primal time for my demons to come out and play.

I could win the jackpot at the nearest slot machine, walk away in swimming in cash, and I would still be so unhappy. Because I know what I want, and it isn't anything material.

More than anything right now, I just want my sanity, because I feel it slowly slipping away as I lose track of what is real and what isn't.

I look back at Henry and scrutinize the details of his face. He is real. He has to be. I have felt him breathing, I have heard the beating of his heart with my head on his chest.

I look to my left and then my right at the assortment of hotels.

Henry once told me, "You can go everywhere in Las Vegas without really having to travel at all—you have Italy and France on the same street!" he says, referring to the Venetian and Paris hotels.

Vegas is one of the most artificial cities ever built, nothing is real at all, and it isn't supposed to be. It's magic, and magic is an illusion. I feel like I am being shown what is behind the curtain, as I wonder if I am real, or as artificial as the lights shining down on me.

Henry rises, "Ready?" he asks—for what I don't know, but I nod.

He walks as if he owns this city, his gait cool and collected and he takes my hand in his. I cling to it for dear life as I try to feel the lines on his palms, the warmth of his skin, and the subtle twitches of his fingers as he tries to make his grip comfortable. Not everything real is horrible, for he lives and breathes.

We take the elevator up, and as we do, my stomach begins to fall into knots. He will sleep, I will not, or will seldom.

As he effortlessly slips into a slumber, I stare out at the city and stroke my scarring wrist in a psychiatric medication induced daze.

I look at Las Vegas and the tiny moving specks that are

people still awake walking up the Strip. They can't see me, but I can see them, and I like it that way. I don't want to be seen. I want to hide.

"What are you doing?" Henry's voice startles me. "Come to bed."

I fall onto the mattress, into his arms, and feign sleep. I didn't answer his question. I didn't want to tell him what I was doing, what I was thinking, what shadows cast themselves in my head.

Because if I told you, my love, of things best forgotten, but that never can be, you would run.

AND YOU THOUGHT THANKSGIVING WAS BAD

July 24, 2019

I am staring at myself in the full-length mirror in the guest room at my mother's home, trying to tie a neat bow around my waist in the dress my father had approved of and bought for me for this occasion.

I wanted to wear black. I liked black on any occasion, but this was a memorial service, and I was more than in mourning. However, the instructions were explicit, "casual California" attire.

"Zak wouldn't have liked everyone in 'funeral fashion'" my stepmother had giggled, pointing at a plain, but elegant black gown at a department store the night before the service. "Can you just imagine how he would feel seeing you dressed in that and your dad in a suit!"

I say nothing in response, but I want to scream at her. She, nor anyone else attending this shit show that has been organized via a Facebook invite as if it were a children's birthday party, know anything about what my brother would have liked.

My stepmother insists that I model an innumerable display of dresses for my father. I hate most of them and I feel like I am both naked and ten years old each time I step out of the dressing room and into his scrutinizing stare.

"No," or "too short" or "it's too tight on your chest" and "absolutely not" are all responses the ensembles garner.

He looks as though he is about to have a heart attack as I

emerge in a black fitted jumpsuit that I picked out from one of the racks when my stepmother was turned away. Next.

One of the last dresses I emerge in evokes a nod and a "yes, I like this one."

The cringing truth I won't admit, is that I do too. The dress is white and tea length and has a pattern of pink flowers with flowing green vines on it. It fits my body well and is conservative without making me look like a maid. As I stare at myself in the fitting room mirror though, it looks far more fitting for a summer picnic than honoring the memory of my brother.

"With a sweater," my father says nonchalantly, as he pays for the dress without further comment.

I thank him but feel a sting of resentment as I do. It is the first thing he has bought me in I don't know how long, and it is only because his son and my brother is dead.

As I ready myself the morning of, I search for a sweater. Tattoos and scarred wrists taint my father's perfect picture, and that will not do.

As my mother and I drive from Orange County to San Diego in silence, I stare at the flowers that adorn the trim of my dress, and I realize that no matter how many roses you try to cover it with, the shit of this family still stinks from a mile away—and no matter what he does, my father's picture he is trying so hard to paint is smeared with it.

I think of the circus that is today, with him, the ringmaster, at the center. Two ex-wives, four stepchildren, wife number three at his side, a dead child, and another who is on death's door. *Smile and nod.* It's only for a few hours.

Before we arrive, I devour two cigarettes and a cup of bitter, lukewarm black coffee. I don't give a shit if I smell like an ashtray. In fact, I hope I do, and that it will deter anyone from touching me, hugging me, or offering their condolences.

As we approach Fort Rosecrans National Cemetery, I see an ocean of white headstones, each marking a serviceman or woman lost. It is a sight I have always both hated and admired, but today I loathe it, as my brother joins the marble abyss.

As I turn my head, I see a collection of cars and people, and I know what they are here for. I silently curse them all and wonder how many of them responded "going" to the Facebook event my father organized. I stare through the car window at them through slitted eyes of seething resentment: my father's former coworkers, random do-gooders from the church he used to attend, people who I know are my family members but who I have not seen in so long I can't remember their names.

And I couldn't bring my rock, I think, as I choke on Henry's absence. I submitted to my father's commands, and now Henry was on his way back to Vegas for his 40th birthday. Another thought that sends me seething. He is gone and gone without me. I should have just stayed in Sin City and let all of my demons loose. Instead I am here.

As people approach me, offer their sympathies, I recoil at even the slightest touch. My father's entourage all approach me, several of them tell me what a lovely girl I have grown into.

"I heard you were getting married," a woman, whose name I forget as soon as she says it to me remarks.

"Not anymore," I bark and walk away. This is hardly the time or place to explain my broken off engagement and new relationship. I retreat to the only bathroom and begin to cry. I will not let the peanut crunching crowd see me crumble. *Not today*, I think, as I try to reapply my mascara between streams of salty tears.

When I emerge, my mother looks annoyed. It is almost time for the service to start and we make our way in a procession to a large white pavilion, where a priest in dress blues is already waiting. I don't see him though. What I see is the canister that is my brother.

I had never really thought about what I wanted done with my body when I died, and I doubted Zak had either. I think that the choice for cremation was one made out of logic and reasoning rather than preference. I had never really given much thought to the process or idea of cremation at all, but here he was, his stocky, 6-foot 1 frame condensed to ash in this....jar...urn...container?

His mother, my father's wife before my mother, had tried to add some life to it, picking out one that had a mural of a sunset on it, but staring at it, all I could think of was death and dying, and vomiting. I had just seen him. He had just slept next to my bedside. He had just hugged me goodbye. Now here he was or...wasn't.

His mother had saved a portion of the ashes for me, and as the service begins, I become overwhelmingly grateful for that. Because this service, or rather this performance, is not for Zak.

I think of staring out at Matanuska Glacier with him, when we were the only people in the world.

"We grew up around the ocean," he ruminated, "but I don't care what anyone says, this is the most beautiful thing in the world."

Everything in Alaska is a postcard, and that moment and those mountains gave credence to that phrase. Yet as I think of my blood that stains a motel room, Carrie's caved in skull, and the pile of ashes in front of me—I think it's beginning to look more like the centerpiece to a tragedy. But I know I will have to go back, because that is where his ashes belong. At that glacier, *our glacier*.

My father is the keynote speaker for the shit show and any semblance of control and calm I have is lost the second he opens his mouth and begins to talk.

I begin heaving in silent, heavy sobs and I can feel people staring at me as my mother rests her hand on my back. It is taking every ounce of willpower I have not to scream and run. At some point God hears my prayers and my father's voice ceases. I feel his eyes burning through me as he returns to his seat.

The crowd disintegrates into factions and I take my crown as the head black sheep of the family—retreating to the road to devour a cigarette. Then I meander further from the people and situate myself amongst the white headstones and stare out at San Diego Bay. I want to throw myself in it, as I make a mental note to inform several people to ensure that my father not speak at my funeral should I die. Which, staring at my wrist, I realize is a very likely possibility.

My mother insists we make a brief appearance for hors d'oeuvres at Zak's mother's house and I oblige but avoid going in for a half an hour as I talk to Henry on the phone.

He is almost to Vegas, and I am stuck here.

"I hope you have a great time," I say through gritted teeth.

I need him here, but it doesn't matter right now. Nothing matters, as I walk into the house and remember that I have been off my Antabuse for ten days now. *Close enough*, I think. *I will take my chances.*

But how?

I avoid everyone and everything and busy myself with the house dog. It can't talk back and licks my hands without judgement or question. I can't help the obsession I have with the half-empty wine glasses the other grievers are holding. My desperation to drink is insatiable and I start making plans.

"To Zak," I announce, raising the Kamikaze that was just ordered for me later that night at a pub down the street from my mother's house.

The drink is down and gone in a few sips and I announce my need for another by slamming the glass on the table in front of me.

"You really are Zak's sister," the idiot I have decided to meet here laughs.

"Yeah," I say, irritated at the comment, "Get me a Jameson."

And he does, and then he gets me another, and another, and I even find myself laughing as I listen to what is likely the worst rendition of Amy Winehouse's "Valerie" on karaoke.

"You gonna get up there and sing blondie?" an intoxicated marine from the local base asks me.

"You'll be attending my funeral first," I say drunkenly, and I realize I need both air and a cigarette.

The night breeze hits me as soon as I am out of the door and I drink it in. My flesh is a bit flushed, but I can't decide if it is a reaction to the medication still being in my system or a sunburn, and I don't care.

Across the parking lot I spot a drugstore, and I have the sudden inclination that drinking on my own would be a much more congenial affair. Before anyone can see me, I sprint to the store and purchase a fifth of Jack Daniel's and have it stuffed in my bag in the time it would have taken to smoke a cigarette.

When I reenter the bar, I order and down one more drink and announce, "I want to go home."

I am the grieving sister. I am not to be questioned. Not tonight. And he doesn't question me. He takes me up the street and back to my mother's within a matter of minutes and tells me he hopes to see soon. I smile and nod but know as I shut the door, I will never see him again.

Instead of entering my mother's house I situate myself on her porch and begin to enjoy the bottle I bought for myself—and I cry. I cry all of the tears I held back during select moments during the day.

Through my blurry vision I spot a potted plant that was delivered to my mother from the Orange County Fire Benevolent Society as a condolence for my brother. My grief turns to rage as I get up and kick the plant over, soil spraying everywhere.

"What. Are. You. Doing?!" my mother says alarmed as she opens the door, her gaze shifting from the toppled plant to the bottle.

My rage transfers from the plant to her as I grab the bottle before she can and storm into the house.

When I awake, it is on the kitchen sink. My shirt is nowhere to be found, and I can tell from the raw quality of my throat that I was screaming. My head is screaming.

I begin to walk towards the stairs and crack the bones in my aching body and then I realize I cannot close my right hand. In fact, I can't feel half of it. Looking down at my fist, the ring and pinky fingers have curled in like gnarled roots. I try to straighten them. Nothing happens.

I groan as each stair feels like a mountain. My mother is staring at nothing as she sits atop her blue bedspread.

I don't apologize. I don't ask what happened.

"Where is my whiskey?" I ask, and for the first time, she doesn't look shocked.

"In the guest room, where you left it," she says, "and you need to leave."

But I barely hear her as I am already making my way to the guest room. I can't even grab the bottle with my demented dominant hand, and clumsily fumble after it with my left, gagging on the warm whiskey as it goes down.

I catch a glance of myself in the full-length mirror I had dressed in the day prior. I am in a bra and jean shorts, smeared mascara stains my cheeks, my right hand is limp against me, and I hold an almost empty bottle of whiskey in my other hand as though it is my child.

Zak's ashes will be spread into the ocean today, and I have decided against going to the event—an abundance of water and people are a recipe for disaster in my playbook. I think of my little portion of Zak that I am responsible for.

Maybe Henry and I can make the trek to Alaska, and I can say goodbye my way, and maybe this will all feel just even the slightest bit better. But as I look at myself in the mirror and the destruction of human flesh I have become, I know that if I ever want to spread his ashes, I will first have to rise from my own.

ROOM 9

August 10, 2019

I flip through the thick day planner Henry bought me for my birthday. It is adorned in the colors of the rainbow and secured by a pink band. Inside are stickers to help add flare to the expectations I am supposed to set for myself. I try to deduce the day as I flip to the month it is—*August.*

August. How the fuck is it August?

The ocean is blue and the bars to the cage are thicker than ever. I do not know what day it is. They are telling me I am going to die. Do I care? I know I should, but I really don't know if I do. I have to find a way to stop this.

I look in the mirror. The hideous, evil mirror. It's cracking oak frame tells me that it is old and forgotten. I take a glance at myself and I want to smash it.

Fuck room nine.

Fuck this detox.

Fuck every room in this goddamn hospital.

Fuck me.

I scurry out of the room like a rabid animal and check the clock. They don't afford me one in my room. It is a reminder that I am institutionalized.

I stare at a nurse with purple hair and wonder if she thinks the hue brightens her patients' days. It doesn't. It makes me think she is trying too hard and that she is superficial and that I hate her too.

7:58 A.M. *2 hours and 2 minutes*. Fuck.

One rule: *Do. Not. Have. A. Breakdown.*

I am way too close now and it is almost time for a smoke break.

I can't control the tears that begin to spill from my eyes, and I return back to the mirror in my room. My skin is peeling from my face like paper and I wonder if I will disintegrate at any second. Perhaps that would be ideal. But I can't, because then I wouldn't make it to 10:00. I have to hear his voice one more time, even if he hates me. I hate me.

I breathe in. Henry. Think about Henry. 2 hours. Breathe in. Breathe out. *Do. Not. Have. A. Breakdown.* I can't stop sobbing.

"Smoke break!" the nurse with the purple hair calls with her high-pitched voice.

Maybe there is a God.

I've made this journey more than once. The first time was at around 2:00 in the morning, during my first detox here— after Zak's death. I had not wanted to come then, and I had not wanted to come now. It was at the end of May, and now it is August. Fucking August.

That first time I had clung to a metal bench outside of the entrance to the ER room. Henry had to pry me off of it and keep watch over me until the hospital staff took charge of me and my mother arrived. And then I screamed and screamed and screamed. My mother had likened my being to demonic possession.

I had stared at that same bench as I came in this time, to the same ER entrance. I passed it meekly, knowing it would not save me from my destination, and I was desperate for help this time.

I didn't have it in me to scream at my mother when she arrived for my third medical detox of 2019. I was too busy vomiting up blood and bile.

"You have to promise you won't leave AMA," the ER nurse told me. "And even then, I don't know if they will let you in. You've left twice."

AMA(against medical advice), because the truth was, I trusted my own advice more and I usually went stir crazy on the final two days of my stay at Mission Laguna.

The paperwork was always the same.

"You risk having a seizure."

I know.

"You risk delirium tremens"

I know.

"You risk death."

I know.

"And we can't be held liable"

I know. Where do I sign?

They had admitted me again though, after I had pleaded with all of the earnestness I had left for them to let me in. I was sure I was going to die if they didn't—and worse, I was out of money and out of resources to afford me the means to drink.

The lead nurse of the floor had heard my story when I came in the first time and would sit with me as I sobbed.

"I've never seen anyone cry so much," she had told me.

Her name was Tina and she looked like a nurse. She had neat blonde hair and a tired, but a kind smile and sharp, piercing blue eyes. Most importantly, she had a collected, calm voice that made everything alright.

On my third day there she had come straight to my room at the beginning of her shift and knocked at the door. I was in my usual position, fetal, staring out at the ocean through blurred tears. I didn't turn when I heard the knock. I did not care to talk to anyone about my eating habits, my bowel movements, my withdrawal symptoms—my brother was dead and that was the only thing in the world I could see or feel.

"It's me," was the noise that turned me around.

Tina was the only person I cared to have any interaction with. I seldom talked back to her, but she would talk to me. I liked her because she never told me that it was going to get better or that it was going to be okay. Rather she told me little stories of her childhood or of her dogs at home. They were simple and altogether meaningless, but real and for brief moments they would drown out the horrible voice in my head telling me that this was all my fault.

"I brought you something," she told me that day, holding out a stuffed brown bear. "It's not much, but I just wanted you to have something."

It was a gesture of kindness, and one I felt thankful for. I thought I would always remember Tina by it, but this would not be the last I would be seeing her.

Now I was seeing her again, in August. Fucking August.

I think of how I came here this time and I realize I will probably be shown no such compassion or patience by any of the hospital staff.

Three days ago, I had come to in a hospital bed—a scene that was becoming a regular occurrence for me. As I tried to focus on my immediate surroundings, the doctors and nurses coming and going, the most illuminating fact was that none of them noticed me. I was not dying, not yet anyhow. But how had I gotten here—again?

The urgent care. I had gone for the withdrawals, which I couldn't handle anymore, but waiting the few hours it was going to take to get anything they would give me to settle my shakes and nerves was going to be far too long, so I had grabbed some wine across the street.

When at long last I saw the doctor, she gave me nothing, likely seeing my history and thinking it too risky to let me detox myself. And then—-and then? I can't remember. My stream of consciousness is interrupted by a knock in the doorframe.

"Hannah?" A middle-aged, bald man asks me. It takes me a moment for me to register that he is a doctor.

I nod.

"Here again," he says. "I just saw you not too long ago."

I can't remember him, but I know he is telling the truth. He glances down at a chart in his hand and shakes his head—I feel as though I am about to be scolded by my father. I can tell he is about to begin to chide me, but before he can begin, I make my case.

"Look—," I tell him, "I'm going to need Ativan, I have a seizure history."

"Yes, I know you do," he says. "But your blood alcohol level is still far too high for us to administer you anything. Do you want to know what it was when you came in?"

He doesn't wait for me to reply.

"399. Your highest yet. You're lucky you didn't go into a coma or die. Someone found you on the floor of a Target and had to call the paramedics. You are going to die if you keep doing this. It is not a matter of if, just when."

The entire spiel—-my blood alcohol, the way I was found,

the death sentence—sends a wave of apathy through me. I am not shocked by any of it, I am not scared or dismayed by any of it, I accept it. What I am, however, is furious at this doctor and the fact that he feels compelled to degrade me without knowing me, what I have been through, and that he will not give me Ativan. I am already shaking.

His dark eyes turn into slits as he reacts with disgust to my slate visage. He says nothing as he leaves the room.

I examine my things. My clothing is nowhere to be found. I find about $80 worth of cash in my purse, but the liquor I had stored in it earlier is, not shockingly, gone. My phone is dead, and I wonder if anyone knows I am here.

A social worker comes later and asks if I have anywhere to go—it becomes clear very quickly that I do not. My mother nor Henry want to take me in the state I am in, not only am I still hopelessly drunk, I am out of my mind. The social worker is the only kind person I have met in my time here and she informs me that while she can't give me a place to go, she can give me a taxi voucher.

"Find me the cheapest motel in Pomona," I tell her, and I begin to calculate the cost of things I will need in my head—a room, a phone charger, and most importantly—more liquor.

I contemplate what happened next as I fall in line behind the other detox patients as we go to the smoke break and I am lost. The familiar, overwhelming desire to die hits me as memories from the past few days flood my conscience.

I left Pomona Valley Hospital in a long-sleeved white shirt and blue sweatpants that were both at least four sizes too large for me, but I made it to the motel. While it was a place to sleep, what it was not was close to any liquor or convenience store. This was problematic.

I settled into my small room, completely absent of any belongings and saw a group of people right outside my door. Two women and two men—they all looked like they were enjoying their night far more than I was.

Both of the girls reclined on a car, wearing cut off jean shorts and fitted tank tops. I wondered if they were sisters. The men smoked cigarettes and talked amongst themselves. I surveyed myself in the large mirror of my room. I looked horrific. My makeup mostly gone or smeared from the day's events, my blonde hair a tangled, frizzy mess, and my small frame being swallowed by the massive hospital clothes. They would surely think I was insane—but at this point, anything was worth a shot. I open the door.

"Hey," is all I say to one of the men, staring at the floor.

"How's it going?" he asks, surveying me.

"Haven't had the best day," I respond, and then I cut to the chase, "Look, I need a really big favor. Is there any way you can take me to the store? I'll give you some cash."

"What kind of store?" he immediately asks.

I don't even try and hide it, as I know my shaking likely gives me up.

"The liquor store."

I look up and he smiles.

"No problem," he says. "My name is Edwin. Is that all you have to wear?"

"My name is Hannah," I say. "And yeah."

"Sylvia!" He barks at one of the girls, "Give her something of yours to put on and be quick about it."

The younger looking of the girls shoots me a quick glance but then walks away and enters a room two away from mine. Edwin opens the door to the car the girls were reclining on.

"Here," he tells me, handing me a red solo cup. "While you wait."

I don't even think about what could possibly be in the cup, if it is drugged, if it is even alcohol, but I eagerly take a sip of it and feel the echoes of relief as I taste apple-flavored whiskey warm my throat.

"Thank you," I tell him, and I mean it with all that I have.

Sylvia returns and hands me a small pile of clothes without a word. I look at her. She is more shapely than me, but is also petite and I figure whatever she has given me will fit me far more comfortably than the massive tarp I am wearing. I thank her and go to change, trading the oversized hospital hand-me-downs for a pair of fitted gym shorts and a white shirt with a cartoon monkey on it. It would not be my first choice of attire, but I make do in it and express my gratitude to the girl, and we all leave.

I feel like a new human being when we return, and I have a handle of vodka in my possession and a phone charger. I am safe. I am going to make it through the night I tell myself.

"If you wanna hang out with us, we have just about any drugs you could want," Edwin tells me and the other girl who's name I have not picked up rolls her eyes.

I smile and nod, telling myself I will just drink with them for a bit. After all, I don't want to be alone, not after today, but I won't be doing any drugs. It's been over three years since I got free from the grip of opiates, and I am not planning to start again tonight, because for those who couldn't tell—I am doing fantastic.

I enter the room they are sharing and am immediately taken aback at how bare my own looks compared to it. There are bags and clothing everywhere, open boxes of half-eaten food, and an abundance of drug paraphernalia. I remind myself I have been in these types of rooms before, it's just been a while, but my anxiety is heightened. Nothing another shot won't fix.

I open the large, glass bottle of vodka and drink straight from it, feeling it burn my insides on the way down and I wonder when the last time I ate was. It doesn't matter. I'm okay.

I plug my phone in and text Henry.

First response: *Have fun with Alex.*

As I watch Edwin fasten a belt around Sylvia's arm and load a rig with who-knows-what, I respond.

I'm not with Alex, I say, and this is true. I'm somewhere much worse and I know what I am about to do suddenly. *I need you to drop my stuff off. Lemon Tree Motel, room 127.*

Even if by chance he does come. He won't find me there.

"Hey," I ask Edwin, as he focuses on the syringe he has buried in the middle of Sylvia's arm, "Do you have black?"

His shit-eating grin becomes a wide-toothed smile.

"Yes," he says. "Yes, I do."

And before I know it, I have a rolled dollar bill in my mouth, tin foil in my hand, and the sharp taste of vinegar on my taste buds and sour smoke in my lungs, and everything I care about goes away. I feel happy. I feel numb. I settle on the bed next to Sylvia. Her head is hanging limply from her neck, and I try to support it with my own.

"It's good isn't it?" Edwin asks me.

I nod.

"Here," he says, handing me a giant mound of black tar heroin, "That's for you."

I contemplate the little rock between my fingers, rolling it gingerly. It must be almost a gram, and I wonder why he is being so generous. I feel good, but not stupid, and eventually make an escape. Henry has left my things at the front lobby. I try to find even an inkling of guilt or remorse for the things I have done, but I cannot.

Instead I return to my room and piece away at the little mound, smoking it until I begin to vomit up vodka and bile. Eventually I sleep.

I awake to morning light and consuming nausea. The guilt I was searching for the night before is crushing me. To avoid vomiting on the bed, I sprint to the bathroom. I feel as though I am going to heave my internal organs out, but all that comes up is a small bit of water and what is very clearly blood.

I need more vodka to think. My body is screaming, doing everything it can to reject the liquor, but I am fighting back, taking in more than I can handle. I suddenly find myself with a fire burning underneath tin foil again, not caring that I am killing myself. I need this to do what I am going to do next. The dreaded call.

He has heard it more than once and it always starts the same: "help." And I really need it right now. He doesn't fail me, he never does, but this time I am given a bleak choice:

"Get in the car. We are going to detox, or you can stay here and die."

I know if I do stay the latter will happen, but before I can leave, I take as many desperate sips of my vodka as I can, and we are gone.

Now I am here. Again. And it is August. *1 hour, 47 minutes.* That is when he said to call. I am sure he hates me, and it is clear why. I hate me. I hate me so fucking much. I want to scream. I want to go home. I want to be out of the prison of my flesh. I want to shatter. I am a fool to think that anyone will want to pick up the pieces.

I leave AMA for my third time two days later.

I am back in Pomona, back with Henry, but how I do not know how. The last day and a half is a blur. I am at the tail end of another bender and I tried to return to Pasadena for what would be my fourth detox of the year—it had only been about two weeks since I had left my last.

I had run out of the bottom shelf vodka I was hiding in different areas of the house and had brought Henry to his knees. I was crying, he was crying. We were supposed to love each other—and in that horrible scene, as I begged him to go to the liquor store and make the horrible agony I was enduring stop, he looked at me with such a sad desperation and then defeat. I knew that he loved me, knew that I could use that to get what I needed, and I hated myself for that. I loved him, I loved him so much, but I needed to silence the voice in my head so much more, and unfortunately that meant collateral damage.

Same deal as always: I want a drink, I am going to the hospital. Fine by me. Just make it stop.

As we drive, I take sips of the concoction of Jack and Coke Henry has made for me, thinking how it won't be enough and wondering if I will ever see him again. At some point he will grow tired of this. I cry and I beg, and I plead. He takes pity on me.

"I want to be your wife, I want a family with you," I blubber in my drunken mess as we coast down the 210 free-way. Even in the state I am in, I know how ridiculous it sounds and how ridiculous I look, contemplating the disaster that is me in the sideview mirror. I am not fit to be a wife; I am barely fit to be human.

"Hannah Camacho sounds nice," he tells me, smiling. And it does, but even I know that this will never come to pass. He is talking to a sad, drunk girl that he needs to get to detox.

Eventually I feel the need to drown out the voices in my head with music and for some reason, Dolly Parton comes to mind. I begin playing "Jolene" from the speakers of my phone as we drive.

"This is a really great song," he tells me, and it is. I play it over and over as we. drive.

> *"Jolene, Jolene, Jolene, Jolene*
> *I'm begging of you please don't take my man*
> *Jolene, Jolene, Jolene, Jolene*
> *Please don't take him just because you can*
> *You could have your choice of men*
> *But I could never love again*
> *He's the only one for me…"*

The words echo through my head, and I think of the way I love Henry. How I have never and never will love anyone like him. But there is no Jolene, no one taking him from me, there is just me and this fucking bottle ruining it all. I take another long sip to try and forget about that and all of the things I want that I will never have as a result of it.

The arrival at the hospital is an ugly one. He has to scream at me to leave the car until I finally do and find myself waiting and shaking in the ER—alone. I think of how if it were anything else, a broken arm, a car crash, even something so little as a toothache, he would be there, holding my hand through it all. Yet I have chosen the bottle, and he cannot bear any more pain, not tonight. I would have left me a long time ago.

The hospital does not admit me to detox. What they do instead is write me a prescription for Librium, to take at home. I don't even try to kid myself that I will be able to do this properly

In some sedative-induced daze, at some point, I have gotten from the hospital, back to Henry and we have decided for me to try and do this detox at my mother's. He won't say it, but the unspoken truth is that I am taking too much out of him. I see it in his face, the sunken in look beneath his eyes—he is exhausted.

To get from my Pomona to my mother's I will take a train and I decide this is a perfect excuse for a couple more drinks, before I really make a last-ditch effort to stop. So begins the ominous negotiation yet again. It doesn't take much now. I have sapped him of his will, of his belief in me. This is us—and it is tragic.

The only drinks we can find near the train station are beer and wine coolers, so I go with the latter, stuffing a few in my bag for the trip. Before I board the train, I open one and down it quickly and give Henry a sloppy, but sincere kiss. I will be seeing him again, I have to. I belong with him, and I try to convince myself he belongs with me, but in my heart I know better.

I situate myself in a seat on the upper level of the train. It is packed but other passengers avoid me as I open another one of my wine coolers. People are staring and I let them. *If they only knew*, I think. But they don't, and to them I just look like a desolate alcoholic. I am starting to realize that perhaps, I am.

The ride to my first stop at LA Union Station goes by in a daze, as I write scrawls and scribbles in my journal between drinks on the way and am not-so-kindly told by a conductor that I need to exit to transfer trains. I am out of alcohol.

As I step onto the platform, I look around the bustling station and remember all of the times I have been here before —-this was always where I would stop on my way to Orange County from Santa Barbara. I wonder what that girl would think if she saw the shell I had become now.

I try to read my ticket and the connecting trains but quickly give up—not looking at the time or caring how much of it I have. If I miss my scheduled train, I will catch another one. Right now, I need a cigarette, and I figure there has to be somewhere I can get a drink here.

I have no sense of direction as the mixture of wine coolers and benzodiazepines makes my head spin. The throbbing sensation is made worse by the masses of people going to and from their destinations; I am stuck among them.

I think back to my times here though and the lonely cigarettes I would have as I was so near to getting back to Alex on my trips home two years ago, and my feet begin to take me away from the boarding area and to the end of the tracks where a collection of isolators take puffs of cigarettes.

I fumble through my purse until I finger a half-filled pack of menthol cigarettes, retrieve one, and light it with a complete absence of obligation. I watch the orange flame ignite the small white cylinder between my eyes as smoke fills my lungs.

It is then that a sudden and overwhelming dichotomy of emotions overcomes me. I want to smoke every cigarette I have left in my pack, and then buy another. I want to smoke until I have lung cancer tonight.

There is another part of me that cannot handle the sickly ash flavor at all, that chokes on it. I do not have the energy nor the desire to even so much as hold the cigarette, let alone bring it to my mouth and inhale from it. It falls from my fingers and topples on the cement railway platform, spraying ash and sparkling embers as it bounces and then rolls away from me. I make no effort to put it out and leave it.

I have a train to catch but have no intention of doing so. Instead I follow a throng of new arrivals to the station who are making their way underground. My suitcase feels like a weight behind me, like the baggage of my life I cannot let go of. As I walk away from the departing trains and further into the station, I am overcome by the hundreds of people. There are so many of them. So, so many. And there is me. Alone. So alone and so apart. I want to scream and break through their ordered chaos.

See me, hear me, know me, understand me. Yet I know in my head, that even if I did, that it would mean nothing, and I suddenly am filled with an overwhelming peace as I stop in my tracks and turn. I do not want a drink anymore. *I do not want to drink.* This is the first time I have felt like this in months and I mean it. I do not want to be drunk.

No, I want to die. I turn around and head back up above ground to the loading station.

More people. They do not know my secret. They do not know what I am about to do, but I do—because the bottom line is, I cannot do, cannot live this life any longer. The idea of breathing for another five minutes seems like an insurmountable task, let alone boarding another train. I deserve peace.

I retreat to a desolate area of the tracks, where there are no people around, but that a train will be departing out of shortly. My motions are mechanical. I arrange my bags in a neat pile—my large black suitcase that has become a symbol of my lack of a true home, my purse that has become nothing more than a stashing area for bottles and pills, and finally, my journal, my beloved journal that has almost three years of my innermost thoughts. It tells a story. A very sad story, I think, and this will be the end of it.

I finger through my purse and hear the clacking of pills against plastic—the Librium.

I'm out of booze but my head is still swimming with the aftermath of the wine coolers and I have another ace up my sleeve. I will not be leaving this up to chance, I am resolute in my decision. I stare at the orange bottle and open it without hesitation, pouring an abundance of the pills into my right palm until they start to spill and fall onto the platform. I make no effort to pick them up as I see that the bundle in my hand will be more than enough for what I am trying to accomplish. I pour them all into my mouth at once and wash them down with water. Despite how many there were, I am surprised at how easily they go down. With that out of the way, I look around and am pleased to still see a lack of activity and I examine the height of the platform to the track. It isn't extremely high, but if I fall the right way, and hard enough, and if the train doesn't see me, and if the pills have enough time to work—I step off the platform.

Darkness consumes me.

When I awake, my entire body is screaming in pain and the throbbing in my head is worsened by ominous beeping from the familiar sound of a heart monitor. I try to move my hands to feel my chest but quickly realize they have been restrained to the bed I am on.

I feel myself breathing and my heart rate quickening. I am very much alive, and this isn't hell, but it isn't heaven either. Where am I? And how am I going to explain this one?

DAS VEDANYA, COMRADE
August 25-October 7, 2019

The next month and a half is what is continually referred to as "Hannah-time". I enter my third inpatient treatment center of the year, after another stay at the psych ward following my failed suicide attempt. I am told this place is for the "severe cases", the place that will take the individuals the other treatment centers don't want to take.

"Lots of people just get sober going to AA meetings," I reason with my case manager during my second week there, as I try to negotiate leaving. I had spent the first week huddled in a fetal position, sobbing in the sun, wearing only Henry's jacket and occasionally changing my yoga pants. I looked and felt like hell.

"Yes," Diana, the woman assigned to my case, agrees with me. "They do. But they don't throw themselves onto train tracks."

I want to scream at her when she says this. I want to scream at everyone in this entire treatment facility, as I am subject to almost daily body checks to ensure I am not hurting myself, constant checks throughout the night to make sure I am breathing, and people consistently asking me if I am okay or want to talk. I beg and plead for a visit with Henry, but am not given one till my second week, and try again to negotiate coming home, but he isn't having it.

"I want to spend decades with you," he tells me, "What is 45 days? How am I supposed to have children with someone who just walks away?"

His sentiment makes complete sense, but it drives me seething and I snap.

"Why are you even here?!" I yell at him, but I think the question really is: "why am I here?".

I was supposed to be dead. Instead, I was back in Orange County, the place where I had grown up, supposedly getting world-class treatment, and I wanted more than ever for that train to have ripped me into a million pieces.

I will not be going home—to Henry's or my mother's. If I want to leave, it will be fully on my own accord and I will be homeless. I know I have a measly near $300 dollars in my checking account, and that that will last me not even a week. I am completely out of friends and cut the majority of my family out long ago.

I weigh my options carefully. If I go out, I need to be intent about death and dying, because I will not last any other way. Henry tells me if I go, to not call him, because he knows my departure will mean my death within a matter of days or weeks. Perhaps hours.

"Can you blame him?" one of the group therapists asks me when I share Henry's resolutions. "Do you really think anyone wants to watch you kill yourself?"

I say nothing but know the answer very well. No one has wanted to watch any of this. I had got tired of watching it, of living it, so I had tried to end it, and I had failed. I examine my predicament.

I can't function in society. I can barely hold a conversation. I can't sleep through the night. I can't drink. I can't do drugs. I can't even kill myself right. I feel like a complete degenerate.

In one of the groups I am pushed into, the leading thera-pist asks us to write about one of our greatest accomplishments. I bite hard on my lip as I put my pen to the worksheet and think of the things I have done.

I have had a child. I graduated college, at the top of my class, by the time I was 20 years old. I have lived on my own since I was 17. I beat the statistics for teen mothers that were set and expected of me. I ran a household. I started a career. I had followed my heart....

....and I had almost lost it all, because I am an alcoholic and completely mentally unhinged. I start to sob as I drop the pen and cease the exercise. My inner self-hatred to my treatment team is extremely apparent.

What they do not expect from me, however, is the change I make after Henry's visit. As I submit myself to the fact that I will be staying the entirety of the program, and I may as well embrace it.

For the next 45 days, I am present during all of my group therapy sessions, I make art projects, I write more than I have in years, I talk about the trauma I was afraid to touch, I even make a friend. Towards the end, I am feeling good, I am feeling a light and a life within me that I thought was gone.

We take multiple outings during my time there and I am always keen to hiding myself under a hood or behind my fellow patients, in case I run into a childhood friend, as we frequent the places I spent my early years. More than that, we seem to go to all of the places where I used to escape with Alex during the blossoms of our relationship so many years ago.

One Friday, the treatment team takes us on a hike in the same place where he proposed to me. I dash away from the group and away onto the dirt path as I feel tears gather stinging my eyes. I will not cry for Alex. *I will not cry for some-*

thing I have let go of, I tell myself. I tell myself this, but the tears flow all the same—and I realize they really are not even for him.

"Where is Aggie?" Hayden had asked me on my last call with him.

Aggie. It was so close to Daddy, but not quite. It was the name Hayden had started calling him early on and it had stuck. Alex was not his father by blood but acted the part from the day he was born, and Hayden loved him with no conception of genetics. That is what made it so hard to say goodbye. I thought of how much it would break my son's heart when we finally had to leave and he wouldn't be able to run into Alex's arms at the end of the day, even when I had long stopped doing so. I knew it would break his little heart, and it did. Almost a year later he wondered where he was and when he was coming back. I did not know how to explain to his five-year old mind that he wasn't and would not ever be.

Time heals all wounds, I try and remind myself, but as I am still tending to the deep scars of my own childhood, I wonder if that is true.

Henry has asked me many a time if I still love him and the question always strikes a nerve. "Of course not!" I want to scream, "I left him, and I chose you. I chose you!" but the answer is more complicated.

I will always love him, worry for him, want him to be okay, but I am not *in love* with him. Things had ended so horrifically though. Our last few encounters being drunken screaming matches, and my eventual moving out after our breakup ending in a black eye and broken furniture. Two alcoholics make for an inferno—our relationship was living proof of that.

Nonetheless, I feel the need, somewhere deep down to say my peace.

I feel the stabbing inclination to wish him well. To leave things on a high note, without bleeding bitterness.

I stare at one of my most recent journal entries and dwell on the first line:

Unfinished business has continually been the death of reason for you.

Yes, this is true and continually talking to and seeing Alex has gotten me nothing but trouble but sitting at the top of this place of a happy memory, I feel the need to say goodbye and goodbye for good and on a good note more pressing than ever. I decide to write it.

So, I do. I spend two weeks going back to four sheets of paper that say all that I have to about my final peace. I do not blame him for one thing in the letter, I do not highlight his faults or misgivings, I do not chide him.

I thank him for so much—for trying to love me in the only way he knew how, for being there for Hayden, for being such an integral part of the most foundational part of my life. I apologize. For breaking his heart, for choosing someone else eventually, for not giving love another chance, for giving up. I tell him to find love, to find family, to find happiness, and to find peace—and to be true to himself.

I end it in a simple fashion, but one that he will understand perfectly well. I imagine him nodding and clenching his sharp jaw as he reads the final words.

Goodbye and good luck.

I don't sign my name, because he knows who it is from. I will mail it to him, along with the stuffed tiger he gave me on our first Christmas together. I remember him handing me the small children's toy that was worn and tattered, holding a small plastic red heart that read "I love you" in faded white letters.

"It was the first gift anyone ever gave me," he told me. "From my babushka."

His grandmother was the only person other than me I ever heard him talk lovingly about, as he would recount a difficult childhood living alone with his father's mother in a small Moscow flat amidst a crumbling Soviet Union before coming to America.

I read it to my one friend and to my therapist before leaving the program.

"It sounds good," my therapist tells me. "You honor him and make a real amends, without making it seem like he has a chance to get you back."

I debate long and hard if I will tell Henry about the letter, as I stuff it in the folds of my planner a day before leaving. Part of me hopes he will find it, so I won't have to bring it up.

I leave on a Friday and spend a wonderful weekend with Henry, eager to get back to real life and start living and living free. I have earned it.

I think of all of the wild possibilities. I can move to the city. I can finally start the book I have always wanted to write. I can go after my dream job. I can see my son again soon. I can get married. I can start a family. I can have a home.

On Monday, I call my son's father to talk with him about seeing Hayden. It will not be happening anytime soon. Before I know it, I am at the checkout of the liquor store and filling a plastic cup with Jack Daniel's.

After a few drinks, I find myself reading the letter I wrote

Alex. It is touching, it is beautiful. It should be read to him, and I should say goodbye to him for good in person, I think.

Within an hour I spot Alex by one of his infamous plaid long-sleeve shirts and cigarette smoke coming from his head.

"Hey," he says. "Make it quick and worth my time."

I produce the letter with drunken pride.

"Let's find somewhere to sit, and then I will go," I promise.

He doesn't know about the whiskey in my purse and allows me two glasses of wine and sips from his beer as I read him the letter, and then a verbal mess of recent writings. This was not how this was supposed to go.

At some point I lose him, I lose time, I lose reality, I lose myself. I come to in a holding cell in the bowels of the Pomona police station.

I've never been good at goodbyes.

PART III
THE BLUE IN THE SKY

WHEN STUCK IN A CELL

October 9, 2019

"Hold out your hands," the nurse tells me. They are still shaking, and I know from experience that they will be for several days.

"We are taking you off of detox," he tells me, "They'll be putting you into a cell."

The ominous "they" wastes no time, and a deputy barks at me to gather my things and get moving.

I examine my things. A bar of soap I have not used, a bent comb, and a blanket with two massive holes in it. I stare at my few possessions, all that I have, and contemplate what feels like the most impossible task as the bones in my body scream.

Instead of picking up my things I look at the deputy in desperation.

"Have I been bailed out?" I beg, not ask. "I'm supposed to be bailed out."

I don't know if this is true or not, but I have to believe that it is, because I cannot be in this place. I am terrified, I am sick, and I feel the overwhelming desire to run, but there is nowhere to go.

"Shut up and get your things," he tells me. "Cell five."

My eyes scan the room until they find a 5 the color of rust over a metal door. I know that once I go through that door it will lock and I don't know if I will ever get out. I start to gather my things into a bundle and realize that it is not just my hands that are shaking, it is my entire being. I can feel my heart fluttering, as though it is ready to burst from fear.

"Please," I whisper, in a last futile attempt.

"GO!" he shouts, and the noise sets me into action and as I walk to the 5 of doom, I wonder if one blanket will be enough to hang myself.

As the door shuts behind me with a bang of finality, I survey my new surroundings. There is a slitted window that is covered in smears of white paint. I press my face as close as I can to it, looking for something, anything, to convince me that the world still exists.

I think I see the fluorescence of what must be a car's headlights as it moves, shifts, and is gone, and then there is only the fog of the paint with a backdrop of darkness. It is nighttime. But how late is it? I realize I have completely lost track of time and question if I even actually know the date.

Aside from the taunting window there are two bunks, a sink, and, of course, a blaring overhead light. I feel a pang of dread as I remind myself that it will not be turning off; not an hour from now, not tomorrow, not ever; I am forever on display.

Finally, there is a mirror, or what is supposed to be one. What it really is, is a buffed piece of scratched metal that is slightly reflective. I look at it for a few split seconds. I avoid my eyes but see the mess of my blonde hair and the open sores on my face. I decide that the metal square is my worst enemy and I get as far away from it as possible into the other corner of the cell, dropping to my knees in a mix of complete exhaustion and agony. I am alone and I am petrified, and I am stuck.

"Help me," is all that leaves my throat as I look to the menacing ceiling light that will stay on for all of eternity. Then I weep, for what feels just as long.

October 12

I stare viciously at the bag of food that was brought to me sometime yesterday and that I have been unable to dispose of. I have not left this cell and I am convinced I am never going to again. The brown paper bag mocks me. I know its contents are warm and the barely edible contents it contains have been made immeasurably worse by sitting. I hate it. I want to rip it apart and scream at it, but I also want it because my body is starving for any sort of nourishment at this moment. However, my showdown with the sack lunch is brashly interrupted by a startling bang on my cell door and the command that has become the only form of communication I am coming to know.

"Last name, last three!" the deputy snaps at me.

I clamor to the door and clutch at nothing as I look at him with frantic eyes. I don't ask the question I have been for the last three days in utter desperation. I am not getting bailed out. In fact, I don't even know if anyone remembers me at this point. No, the question I have is much more pressing.

"What time is it?" I beg, because I need to know, have to know.

"Last. Name. Last. Three," he repeats. He looks like he at me like I am a wild beast, like I am trash.

I break into a sob.

My expectations, like me, are shattered that day though, as I am finally moved from the holding block and placed into a line of other inmates to be sorted into permanent housing. A female deputy viciously chucks a stained yellow shirt at me and commands me to go change—I'm being sent to the mental health module.

Walking to an empty cell to trade out my brown, sweat stained jail uniform, I finger at the yellow shirt, a bright, neon reminder that not only have I been deemed a criminal, I'm crazy too. I want to sob, want to scream, tell them that I'm sane, but thinking on the past few months of my life and staring at the mess of purple and white scars on my left wrist, the stark realization that my efforts will be futile punches me in the gut. I change and accept my fate.

I remember how horrific I thought the psych ward was, with the likes of characters like Lloyd the Egg Prophet and Chris the Creep. Yet in this moment, I would trade anything to be back at that place, sopping up those greasy eggs, for the blaring looks of hate and disgust the deputies are giving me, to not have to go to the new cell I will be assigned. At least there, there was the chance of running away. At least there, I could see the trees outside my window. At least there, I could walk more than three paces of endless insanity. At least there, I could drink water, fresh water, from a cup, and not from the sink of a cell. At least there, there was hope of an end in sight, hope of something else. At least there, I had someone to save me. At least there, I thought that was the worst the nightmare could delve. I breathe and I think back as the other prisoners and I begin to walk, because I have to be somewhere, anywhere else in my mind, to have the capacity to move forward.

LLUVIA, LIKE RAIN

LLUVIA, LIKE RAIN

October 12, 2019

"I'm Hannah," I say in a hushed tone, as I stare at the bottom bunk I have thrown my minimal possessions onto. My taking of it seems like an act of dominance but is really desperation. I have to sleep.

"Lluvia," is all the quiet, chubby girl says, her thin black hair covering her eyes.

"Like rain?" I ask, looking up.

She nods.

It strikes me that I will be spending 23 hours a day in this confined space with this girl. I scrutinize her profile as she looks longingly out the small window of our new cell—number 17. She is stout and fleshy, and her thin, stringy black hair falls over her hooded gaze. Her eyes are like small hollows behind the ebony strands. She emanates the fear that beats through me and I feel drawn to her for this.

Lluvia, like rain. She looks as though she has been drowned. I make it my mission to try and pull her up, find out what is beneath.

I curl up in a ball on my bunk, on the square of plastic and foam that is supposed to serve as a mattress. Pressing my hands against the mat, I cringe as I feel the metal baring under it and can already feel the pain radiating through my back. I try not to think of sleep, of the aching that is still pulsating through my body and just focus on the girl.

I hesitate but ask the question that she is likely expecting. The question everyone is asked.

"What are you here for?"

She continues to stare out the window but after a few seconds, takes a quick glance back at me and relaxes her tense posture.

"I stabbed my husband," is all she says.

The comment shocks me. She looks so fragile, soft, and docile, but before I can ask questions, she continues: "I was off of my meds and we got into an argument. I cut his pretty deep into his arm and he had to get stitches."

I feel like there is more to this story, but this seems to be all she wants to tell for now and I remind myself that I will have hours upon hours of time with this timid girl.

Like an offering of camaraderie, I decide to tell her why I am sharing this cell with her without her asking. I haven't looked at my face but from the tenderness in my jaw, I know it is still bruised, and the open wounds on my wrist and shoulder are incriminating.

"I assaulted a police officer," I say, adding— "apparently. I have no recollection of it. I was drunk. I am an alcoholic."

I feel as though the final admission gives me some sort of reprieve, as well as an identity in a place where I have become nothing more than a number. While that is the question that you are asked by anyone in this place, deputies and inmates alike, I realize there is another unsaid, but obvious question that will permeate throughout this area of the jail alone.

"Why are you in the mental health module?" I ask.

After the words have already left my mouth, I realize there is not a way to ask this question without making it sound horrific. It essentially means: *are you crazy?* But I know we are both wondering this about one another.

"I'm schizo-effective," she says and that's all.

From my brief college education in psychology, before I switched my major to English, I recall that this means the individual can present symptoms of schizophrenia such as hallucinations or delusions, but with less frequency or intensity. If she is anything like me, I know she is not receiving her medications. She looks at me, asking without speaking the same question. I show her my wrist as an act of vulnerability, but before I let her look too long, I retract and cover my arm and speak.

"I tried to kill myself in August," I begin and motion back to my wrist, "But not like this. I told them about it when I was booked."

After a while she sits on the stool that is adjoined to the metal desk at the end of our cell. She begins to talk, really talk.

I learn that Lluvia has three daughters and that her husband, Ronie, who she is not actually married to, is an alcoholic like me. Her life is one of being misplaced—-she grew up in and out of foster homes until she found Ronie at 17. They've been scattered around Los Angeles ever since.

I begin to tell her about my life too. I talk about Hayden, about Henry, and I touch on my struggles with substances, but falter back to family life as I can tell the subject is one she cannot relate to. As I am talking, we are both startled by a pop and look to see that our cell door is ever so slightly ajar—open. We both look at each other, silently asking if we should go forward. I do and press on the cold metal door ever with a gentle nudge and peak my head out.

"Bottom tier!" the deputy calls out, "You have one hour to program. Keep the noise down or you will be sent back to your cells."

With the announcement, a stream of neon yellow begins to pour out of the cells and scatter across the module. I don't even think—I run to the phone. I need to hear his voice, now. It has been days.

To connect the call feels like an eternity, but finally I hear him, and his voice fills me with tears. I would do anything to be with him right now.

"Hello?" he says.

"Henry?" I yelp.

He affirms it is really him and while I want to simply say that I miss him, that I love him, that I need him—a chaotic mess of verbal garbage spews from me as I try to communicate my fear, my anxiety, my desperation.

He confirms what I already know—I am not being bailed out. It is a chance he nor my mother is willing to take. I feel a pang of betrayal, of anger, but I remind myself how I got in here and it dissipates and is replaced by crushing remorse and guilt. The conversation feels so rushed, I know this is the only time I have to shower, to get anything outside of my cell done —but this is what I need. His voice recharges the little energy I have left, gives me life, and propels me to go on for just one more day.

I promise to call him tomorrow as I see the clock nearing the end of the hour and I tell him I love him probably a dozen times between heaving sobs. I leave the payphone in shambles, wrecked at the fact that I am barred from the one I love most, in these walls, with no end or escape in sight. The thought makes me want to die.

As I sob and walk towards nothing, a hand touches my shoulder and I turn to see a gentle-looking, middle-aged woman smiling at me. Her auburn hair has been arranged in a neat bun atop her head and I can tell she is wearing mascara. By jail standards, she looks very well put together.

"I'm Tammy," she says and as I look at her ivory skin that is so palpable amongst the other girls, I realize she is the only other white woman I have seen in the module.

"Hi," I mutter, wiping the mess of tears and snot from my face.

"I heard you were looking for a book," she begins. "It's really easy. You read a book and just ask around the module if anyone wants to trade when you are done."

It's true. When they were sorting us into cells earlier, I had asked about books. It was one of the few things I was excited about in moving to my permanent housing. I would be able to get lost in someone else's world and escape the hell of my own.

She holds out a thick novel with a black cover and hands it to me.

"Here, I'm not going to read it. It will get you started."

I greedily take the book and caress it, feeling the beveled letters of the title, running my fingers between the pages. This is the best gift anyone could have given me in this moment. I want to throw myself at this woman's feet and thank her. This once simple commodity I had has become my greatest treasure.

I hug the book to my chest and tell her, "Thank you."

"Of course," she says and begins to walk away and then turns back, "Oh! I almost forgot. Do you need a Bible? I have a New Testament you can keep."

I don't hesitate, "Yes, please—" because I so desperately need to figure out what God is trying to say to me.

She retrieves a small, blue booklet-looking Bible from her bunk and gives it to me with a smile. I examine the gold letters that adorn it.

New Testament. Psalms. Proverbs.

It's not the whole thing, but it is a start, and I mutter a silent prayer of gratitude for my new gifts, for Tammy.

Before she goes, I ask her the question that has been on my mind for days.

"Is there anything I can write with?" I ask.

She cocks her head and looks at me in a diluted exhaustion.

"You have to order pencils through commissary," she tells me.

Yet another woman interjects the conversation and offers me the stub of a pencil and two sheets of paper. I hold on to these things and my new book with fierce preservation.

I am going to get to read. I am going to get to write. *I am going to get to write.* The thought terrifies but enthralls me, and for a brief moment I think I feel a pang of joy. I must tell Lluvia of my acquisitions, so I return to 17.

Lluvia very quickly became my shoulder to cry on—and I hers.

Tammy went into drug induced psychosis a few days later, and we never saw her again.

LLORONA

I loathe this place with a seething resentment. The floor, the walls, the sink, the table, the deputies, the claustrophobic, ice cold air, and the women. In my head I tell myself I am not one of them. I am college educated, I have a career, I have a good man to go home to—these are all half-truths that I aggrandize. Most importantly, however, I am not a criminal. I convince myself of this.

These girls need this place—they have been here two, three, some of them almost ten times. I will not be returning. I promise myself I will die before that happens, simulating the image of myself slashing my wrists before I am able to be dragged back to jail. That will show them.

In the time I have had to stare at the wall and count the bricks in my cell, I believe I have come to understand the function of jail. The copious amounts of idle time, the 23 hours a day you are stuck in your small, sunless square, you have no choice but to sit with yourself and think about what you have done.

"Shame on you," the white walls say, but for what?

Because as I sit, and think and think and think, the guilt is crushing, but it is not for the crime I am behind these bricks for. It's for everything else I have done. The people I have hurt. My son, Henry, my mother. The sheer fact that my mother had to come see her daughter in prisoner's garb across a glass barrier, sobbing and pleading like a little girl.

Behind all of the hatred and self-loathing, and the madness

that I felt I continued to slip into, I feel like a child. I wanted my mother to scratch my back as she had when I was little and couldn't sleep. I wanted a stuffed animal to hold onto, to feel the soft plushness of something against my cheek. When I grew weary of writing, I drew atrocious, artless sketches of little stick figure families—my family, that I wanted to have.

I sit day after day staring at the cracks in the brick, thinking of the cracks in me, and I try to color them in with the graphite of my pencil and I begin leaving messages, as though their imprint will make me real. I wonder who will see them, if anyone will, as I feel like I will be in this cell forever.

I pray. I walk. I cry. I read. I pray. I write. I cry. I draw. I walk. I pray. I read. I walk. I cry. I pray. I pray. I pray.

"Please God," I murmur. I've already asked for mercy 1,000 times today so now I just ask, "Don't let me lose my mind."

There is one thing and one person, I do not completely despise in this place, the phone, for it is my only connection to Henry, and Lluvia. The marshmallow-faced girl and I have developed our own routines to try and retain sanity.

I had been sitting outside of the infirmary two days ago on the third day of an excruciating kidney infection, keeling over in pain. A woman from my module, with firetruck red hair, who must have been pushing 80 asked me what I was in for. I told her.

"Oh," she said. "You'll be out in no time. I'm on my way to prison for the third time. Spent five years there the last time. I just need to get the hell out of here."

By *here* she means county. For many of the inmates, the future of prison is a welcome one, compared to the bleak reality of 23 hours a day stuck in a cell. Prison promised space, air, sunlight, routines that were set for you.

"This place," she snorts, shaking her mess of frizzy red hair. "If you don't come in crazy, you'll go crazy."

Her words reverberate through my ears throughout the day and I think of how I came in. A drunken, suicidal ball of flesh and fear—and now, and now? Am I much different? I have learned to adapt in many ways.

"*Llorona*", the girls call me, for the. infamous, incontrollable sobbing that takes place on a regular basis during programming hours or on my way to get medication in the mornings. Lluvia takes pity on me though.

The first time she hugged me, I realized the true value of human contact. I grasped onto her for dear life and sobbed into her chest. She would hold me many more times in that cell, and I would hold her too—as we clung and clawed at sanity and at the thought of freedom.

The tears did not stop though, as I gave credence to my nickname of "the weeping woman". My sobs become a soundtrack in the dinner line, on my way to get medication, from the air holes of my cell, and Lluvia always seems to have a gentle hand on my back. It isn't much, but it is something in this hell, and little morsels are worth gold. You take what you can get, and you cling to it here.

We never come up with a name for it, or draw attention to the necessity of the habit, but Lluvia and I begin devising different ways to bide our time throughout the day. We make lists of our dreams, what we wanted to do in the next year, five years, ten. She wanted to go to New York. I wanted to go to Paris. She wanted to go back to school. I was determined to finally write a book. She wanted one more child. I wanted two or three. At one point, we even distracted ourselves devising a long list of baby names we both liked. We talked about our dream weddings—the dress, the colors, the location. It was all the things of fairytales, but it let us laugh and smile for even just a few minutes at a time.

I began making word search puzzles for her, and soon some of the other girls. She would pick a subject and I would use my vocabulary to devise a word bank. The first one was made up of different cities in California and took me over an hour to make, but very soon I got fast at making them and Lluvia helped me make ones in Spanish for some of the girls she had made friends with. My skin color and my timid nature put me at odds with just about everyone, but her hand and my little gifts to the other girls gave me some welcome.

The most agonizing thing was the endless, everlasting time. Each day was a mission to make it to dinner as we would take turns longingly staring at the clock. For some reason, it felt like if we made it to that point, another day was complete, and we had survived. At dinner we would burst from our cells and both creep to the very back of the line of women—to get the most time out of our confined box. Before each meal we clean the days papers and books off the metal desk. She sits on the stool and I sit on the edge of my bunk as we say a quick, but earnest prayer. We then both look up and laugh at whatever slop they have deemed edible for human consumption, sometimes giving names to the meals if they are truly horrific. But it is a time of joy for us. We have made it another day, which means we can make it one more —somehow.

A DISGRUNTLED JUDGE, NO JURY, AND A LUSTY EXECUTIONER

October 19, 2019

The click of the cell door opening immediately jars me from the half-sleep state I am in. I jolt up and see the green uniform of a trustee—a sentenced jail inmate who has been given the "privilege" of a job. The young girl looks surprisingly happy for being up in the middle of the night and greets my grogginess with a warm smile before looking down at a single sheet of paper in her hand.

"Hannah?" she asks. "You have court today."

She doesn't have to tell me that—I know this. I've been waiting two and a half weeks for this day. Two and a half weeks of agony. Two and a half weeks of praying on my knees for answers, for freedom, for mercy. Two and a half weeks of hell.

"Yes," I respond to her. "Is it time to go?" I begin collecting my things.

"No, no," she says. "Just doing a count. It's only midnight. They'll wake you up in about three hours. Get some sleep, and good luck today, I'll pray for you."

Her kindness touches me, and I am so internally grateful for her and the prayer I hope she says in that moment. What her visit has not done, however, is qualm my anxiety. I am not going to go back to sleep. I can't. Not yet anyway.

I begin to pace. Telling myself what I always do—that I will go the length of the cell and back 25 times. I always lose count as I become lost in thought and possibilities within my endless strides from wall to wall. Sometimes I will hit the different surfaces of the cell to see what sounds they make as I walk. Other times I will begin to sing a song that I promise myself I will listen to when I am out. During some walks I get lost in daydreams of what it would be like to be out, to be with Henry, with my son, to be free. Sometimes I feel as though I am walking down to the gates of hell and vanishing into the nightmares of my mind that are so deafening. I do these things until I realize I have lost count and I start over again, trying to get to 25, but never doing it, for my mind always takes over and the cycle continues until my legs grow tired or Lluvia interrupts me.

Yet right now, Lluvia is fast asleep, completely ignorant to my existence, and my mind is racing and wild. So, I walk.

I try to look at the clock through the window of my cell several times, but it is too dark in the outside room. Knowing the time is a luxury here, and it is one I cannot ask for at the moment. It is me, myself, and God once again.

At some point I do lie back down but my brief doze is interrupted by the now familiar popping sound my cell door makes when it opens. It is a sound I wait for with eager anticipation every day; it is the sound of meager freedom. Now it signals that it is time for me to begin preparing for the day ahead.

I retrieve my recycled Gatorade bottle that I use for holding beverages. The plastic has grown stained and murky from my repeated use of it. I spoon in three heaping scoops of instant coffee into the bottom of it and wait until the water in my sink reaches a tepid, lukewarm state and make myself what is supposed to be morning coffee. It tastes like dirt and the undecided temperature of the water makes it entirely nauseating, but the rush of caffeine is one of the few luxuries that I have in here, so I drink.

It's been 21 days, I realize. Please let it be the last day. Today could be the day I go home. That I get released on my own recognizance, if the judge deems me worthy.

I fall to my knees at the edge of the bunk and I pray. I beg God for mercy and for home. I swear to never touch another drop of alcohol again, I swear to live righteously, to be a good mother, a good woman, a good wife eventually. I swear to help people. I swear to be honest, to be modest, to be kind, to be forgiving, to be pious. Just *please* let me out of this hell.

A week ago, I had gone to get my morning medication in a fit of tears. An elderly black woman with kind eyes asked me why I was always crying.

"I'm just sad," I had responded, and: "I don't want to be here."

"The nightmare is going to end soon," she told me, and it felt like a promise, like God was talking through her.

I hoped that today was the end of the nightmare.

It is time to get ready. Compared to my typical routine, this won't be much. I stomach the mirror, only looking at myself through my peripheral vision. My face has healed mostly, but I still look a mess—hollow and afraid from what I do see. I fasten my blonde hair into a neat as bun as I can with a tie I have fashioned from the elastic of standard-issue women's underwear. I had washed my hair the day prior. Lluvia had helped me as she always did, as we washed it in our cell sink so I would not have to waste time in the shower doing it. Every second out of my cell was a precious moment I could have hearing Henry's voice—to hell with my hair.

I then began to put on the only cosmetic product I had—a

bit of mascara that could have been found in the bargain section of a drugstore. It was unlike the expensive tubes I bought from department stores, and made my lashes clump together if I did not let it dry in between coats.

This was as good as it was going to get. I thought of how beautiful I had been, could be. Of the nights I had my hair curled, cascading over a shoulder, my makeup pristine. I had often felt like one of the most eye-catching women in a room depending where I was. And now I looked like I had been dragged down Skid Row by my hair and made a futile attempt to put myself back together last minute. I am suddenly also acutely aware of the yellow of my shirt, and the message it conveys. *I have mental health problems.*

No shit. Normal people don't find themselves in the kinds of situations I have in the past year. But I have made a resolve to myself and to God though that I am done with it all. I just want to go home.

When I am ready as I can be, I exit my cell and head to the front of the module. I am told to wait. No matter what the outcome is, I am filled with excitement over the amount of freedom I will have today. I will get to be out of my cell, out of this module, out of this jail. I may even get to see the sun.

We sit in the dark for a long time, but eventually are transferred downstairs, walking in a single file. I know none of the women from my module who are also going to court. Only two of them are going on the same bus as me I realize as we are squeezed into a small holding cell with around 25 other girls. As they shut the door to the cell, the heat begins to rise, and the air becomes thick. There is a pregnant inmate in the corner of the cell, hovering her head over the metal toilet. I ruminate on how claustrophobic and nauseous I feel in this space and feel a pang of pity for the girl.

I am not going home today. I can tell every girl in this room that I will be, but all of me knows that I will not be seeing the inside of the wood walls of Henry's home. I will be seeing my cell and Lluvia asking me what happened.

Sitting in the holding cell at the Pomona Courthouse, my premonitions have come to pass, as my court date will be extended almost another month and a half. I want to scream.

My attorney asks the judge plain and simple for me to be released on my own recognizance or for my bail to at least be minimized.

The stoic judge looks at me with disgusted, irritated eyes and I look for my mother in the crowd. She is looking at him.

"Due to the public safety concern, bail will remain at $50,000," he announces and that's that.

I have to clench my teeth to keep my jaw from dropping.

Public safety concern? I am not a bad person. I am a college graduate. I am a mother. I am a partner. I am a professional. I am....

Accused of two felonies. And, according to my neon shirt, I am mentally ill in the eyes of the state.

But I swallow as I remember, it doesn't matter. Henry promised that if I wasn't released today, I was getting bailed out, and I know, if anything, that Henry is true to his word.

I had looked forward to being away from my module, but now all I want is to go back, to find out if my bail has been posted, so I am happy when they tell me I will be returning on the earlier bus of the day.

I go down with two of the other inmates and am immediately greeted by whistling by the barrage of male prisoners that are in the middle and back of the bus. We are being seated in a section of the bus between them.

One of the girls who is with us is seated in an individual holding area. She is shackled and is wearing the infamous Velcro gown that is given to inmates who are on suicide watch. I watch her as she sways to the country music that is playing on the half-broken speakers of the bus and starts screaming about her father molesting her as a child. I shut my eyes and try to drown out the sound of her shrieking and the whooping men as I sink into my cold, hard seat. I am startled by a tapping on the glass partition in front of me.

"Hey," a man says.

He is mustachioed and is tattooed from his neck to his face but is calm amongst the chaos of the rest of the bus.

"Hi," I mutter, looking down.

"You don't look like you belong here," he laughs. "What'd you do? Vandalize something?"

I wish, I think, and I tell him my crime. He finds my dilemma comical.

"You'll be fine," he assures me. "You've got beautiful eyes. You know, you're probably the last girl I am going to see before I go to prison."

I am astounded anyone finds anything beautiful about me right now, but I smile, and nod and I ask him the ominous question, "What are you here for?"

The answer shoots a wave of ice through me:

"Murder."

"Oh," I answer.

"Yeah," he begins. "They wanted to give me the death penalty, because they said it was execution style, but I am going upstate."

He says it so nonchalantly that I am astounded.

Before I can process the information, he starts again, motioning at my yellow shirt, "So what, are you crazy or something?"

"No," I say, not believing the answer myself anymore.

"My name is Joseph," he says, "Joseph Quintero."

I nod. Not offering my own name.

"Can I see what's underneath there?" he asks, motioning at the yellow shirt again.

I immediately violently shake my head and realize the rest of my body is shaking. The other men are staring.

"What's your name, sweetheart?" he asks.

I say nothing.

"Name!" His voice grows louder.

"Hannah," I barely say.

"I gave you my full name, what's yours?"

I say nothing.

He bangs on the glass and I look frantically for a deputy, for anyone, but the bus is in motion and I am alone. His banging grows fiercer and I feel tears developing in my eyes.

"Just tell him your fucking name!" one of the girls behind me barks.

"Hannah Camacho," I say, in a panic. It is not the first time I have used my name with his while in custody, omitting my entirely European last name.

Lluvia had been the first to suggest it, noting that it may help me mesh easier with the Latina girls she had easily coalesced with. After a few days, they had let me into their circle as well, and I felt a sense of security as I walked around knowing that I was not entirely alone. But now I was using his name as something to cling onto. *Henry*, I thought. Please. Keep me safe now. I need you.

But he couldn't. He wasn't here. I had to keep me safe. I look down at my wrists and realize that I have used their small circumference to my advantage before and I slip free from my cuffs and make my way five seats back, avoiding the executioner's gaze all the while. When we finally arrive at our first stop, the men's central jail, I return my hands to the shackles and go back to my seat.

The lusty executioner eats me alive and undresses me with his eyes as I walk past him towards the exit.

"I'll be thinking about you when I get back to my cell tonight, Camacho," he says with a fierce knocking his fists against the cage that separates him and I.

The motion springs me into a haste and I exit the bus as fast as I can, taking as many breaths of fresh air as I can before I am sent to yet another holding cell for the time being.

You think about me, Quintero, think about me all you want, but you're going to prison for life, and I am going home.

ALWAYS SAVE SOME SUNSHINE FOR LATER

October 30, 2019

The waiting game has started and every second feels like an hour. I keep returning to the small window at the front of my cell to get a glimpse of the clock. Will it be today? Tomorrow? Ever?

Before leaving the courthouse, I had phoned Henry from the holding cell and informed him of the outcome. He didn't seem surprised and assured me he would get started on posting my bail. Now, back at Lynwood, the question I had first asked during the first few days of my stay here has returned each time a deputy comes by my cell for count:

"Has my bail been posted?"

Some of them laugh at me, some of them give no answer at all, but finally, Deputy B., one of the kinder officers, tells me she will check. Her lack of an immediate return churns my stomach. Another deputy does return for Lluvia though. She has been sentenced to three months, and her good behavior has earned her a bunk in the coveted, open space of the day room—a shared dormitory space with two televisions.

"I'm happy for you!" I tell her, and I am.

It's the best thing she can ask for with the situation she has been given. As for me, I wonder what the best thing I can hope for is.

My next court date has been scheduled for December 12th. So, if I stay out of trouble, at the very least I will get to be home for Thanksgiving, which is more than I could have imagined or hoped for a few days ago. I hold onto the promise I have made myself everyday though: *I will never be coming back here. Under any circumstance,* and I stare at my scarred wrist.

Lluvia collects her few things in a haste and looks at the collection of makeshift decorations we have put on the wall: a clipping from a contraband newspaper of a sugar skull in Dodger blue with baseball eyes, a sticker from a burrito wrapper that reads "say no to drugs", and an assortment of paper hearts Lluvia has folded in our copious spare time.

I almost ask her if she wants any of it, but I realize what a ridiculous question that is. At the end of the day, it is all trash. Instead, I hug her hard.

"You'll be out soon," she promises me, and I hope she's right.

Once she leaves, I am stuck with myself in the cell and realize how quiet it is without her there. The complete absence of noise makes me uncomfortable and makes the monstrous thoughts in my head fester, so I begin to sing, loud, uncaring of who hears my horrific rendition of "Bohemian Rhapsody".

It isn't loud enough to drown out my head though, and eventually I break down in a feverish fit of sobbing and prayer.

"Please God," I beg. Please what?

I had always coped well under the notion that if it ever got bad enough, at least I could kill myself. At my last treatment center, a therapist had honed in on the faulty nature of this coping skill and told me it was time to get new ones. Did she expect this though? Probably not, and right now I had to cling to anything to retain my sanity.

Then, like a floodgate, my eyes begin overpouring with salty tears and the silence is broken by my heaving sobs, as the past year flashes through my brain.

My baby is dead. My sister-in-law is dead. My brother is dead. In an overwhelming way, I feel dead. I grieve for the part of me, that I know after all of this, is gone forever.

My weeping is interrupted by a knock on my cell door.

"Hey," a voice says, and I look up to see that it is Deputy D., so I don't scream or fight back. I remember fondly a day when he saved my fingers from being broken by another deputy's foot and muster a half-smile at him from my swollen face.

"You're going home," he says. "I bet half these girls wish they had a boyfriend like yours."

Then I am weeping again, but out of joy.

"Thank you, God!" I scream and my cell door is popped for me to undergo a psychological evaluation with a mental health professional, a formality before as my being an inmate of the mental health module.

His name is Ray and he has kind eyes and a gentle demeanor. He is one of the kindest people I have met in my 22 days here in just two minutes of talking with him.

He looks at paperwork detailing me and lets out a half smile and a laugh.

"I have to admit, you aren't something I see very often."

"What do you mean?" I ask.

"No prior record. A home to go back to. A career. College educated. Not our usual."

I nod with a sense of pride that is quickly overtaken by shame, and he senses it.

"But you know what," he begins, "I was sitting right where you were, 25 years ago. Been sober since. If I can do it, anyone can do it."

The last line is one I have heard numerous times before

from men and women in treatment centers, in the rooms of 12-step groups, at psychiatric facilities, and more, but for some reason, when they come from Ray's mouth, sitting across from me at this table in the middle of the module, they mean something. They are the nudge of hope that I need in this moment.

"Thank you," I say, and I mean it.

"No problem," he says. "And good luck. Don't come back here."

Don't plan to, but then again, does anybody?

I am allowed a phone call and ring my mother, who I am surprised to find, is already near the jail, waiting for me. Relief floods through my veins and within an hour I am escorted, with two other inmates from my module, downstairs to a holding cell to be released. The walk down and through processing is the most I have moved in almost a month and feels liberating. Feeling my legs glide, it feels as though every step is forward, and I refuse to look back.

The other inmates and I are moved from one holding cell to another, and an older feeble-looking woman with striking blue eyes tries to start a conversation with me.

"This has been hell," she begins.

"Tell me about it," I laugh. "But it's over."

"You know what I got sent here for? An unpaid metro ticket from five years ago! I teach interior design at UCLA and they threw me in here, for that."

I think of how ridiculous that is, how I do not belong here, and how much more so this woman does not. I feel freed by the fact that I am leaving, but she still looks terrified, so I strike up something that I know is familiar: academics. I begin to tell her about my own education in the UC system, my writing, and then, a shout.

"You better shut up, or I won't hesitate to send you right back up to the cell you came from," a female deputy barks.

You can fucking try, I think, before I check myself and shut my mouth. We all sit in silence until the clothing we arrived in is returned to us.

My jean shorts, a fitted gray t-shirt, and a thong with butterflies on it are all that are handed to me. No shoes, no bra, nothing to give me any sense of decency. As I slip on the scant outfit I have, I feel naked as I am cold, and my breasts easily show through the thin shirt.

"Where are your shoes?" a deputy asks, looking at me like I am trash.

Good question, but I sum up the only plausible answer, "Probably in evidence at Pomona PD."

"Checks out," she says looking at my paperwork, and shrugs me off.

My charges do not make me well liked here. I do not fight with her, try to argue that I was intoxicated, defend my actions. It is what it is. I am going home and will forget her face within the hour, and she will forget mine.

After what seems like hours, we are walking up a flight of stairs and I see the flash of my mother's blonde hair and run to her and hug her—really hug her. My time incarcerated has reminded me that I still need a mother, that I still have one. Our relationship isn't perfect, never has been, but we love each other, and right now, I just need her.

We head to the property desk to retrieve my things, but the items wrapped in a manila folder are scant—hair extensions, my bra (as it apparently could be used as a weapon in the holding cell), and my two handmade beaded bracelets.

The first bracelet has Hayden's name in white beads on one side and Henry's in red on the other. The other is a simple four beaded string that I wear above it with two angel wings and the letters "ZJC"— Zachary James Cloe. I carry the things I love, alive or dead, with me wherever I go.

I slip the bracelets back on right away and feel a piece of my identity come back. My mother protests that she needs to use the restroom before we go, as the drive back is a long one. I don't know if that is true, because I still really don't know where I am, but I nod and tell her I will wait. Yet, as soon as she is gone, I can't. It's been 22 days and from the bottom of the stairs I can see the sunlight pouring in from above.

I sprint up the stairs and run out the glass doors and into a pavilion and take feverish breaths of oxygen. The air tastes sweet, fresh, and intoxicating, and I let it fill every corner of my lungs. Then I look up. The sky is a magnificent blue. It is so big and vast and for a second, I ponder if it is real. How could all of this still have existed while I was in that little box? Yet here it was, all still standing, the air still blowing, the sun still shining, the people still being—but somehow it was as if everything in the world had been swollen and electrified. I let it surge through me.

"Thank you, Jesus." I say, as tears fall from my eyes and I remember the words of David I had clung onto throughout my time in my cell.

His steadfast love endures forever.

And right now, in this moment of existential freedom, I feel the love of God, I feel mercy, I feel hope.

"Ready to go?" I hear my mother ask, and I am. I am ready to leave this place and never see it again in my entire life.

That night, despite my best intentions to keep away from nicotine, I buy a pack of cigarettes. Something about the taste of smoke just seems like freedom to me, and I wait for the perfect moment.

The moon is full and brilliant that night and I walk to the park nearby my mother's house, feeling my feet hit the ground with every step. This wide-open space is completely mine, which is both enthralling and terrifying.

I find a bench where I hope no one can or will see me and very slowly bring the flame from my lighter to the tip of the cigarette and inhale. Right away, I feel the rush go to my head, as I haven't in years, and I savor it, closing my eyes and sinking into the wood of the park bench.

When I open my eyes, I stare at the sky, and for the briefest moment I see something fly across the black canvas of the night—shining and glimmering. Whether it was a star, a satellite, or an airplane, I don't know, and in that moment, I don't care. I make a wish, and I cling to it.

"I just want to be happy, and I just want to be free."

IF YOU RUN 1,000 MILES IN A CIRCLE, HAVE YOU GONE ANYWHERE?

December 5, 2019

The sight of children has begun to both sicken and sadden me and they seem to stick out wherever I go. I see them clinging at their mothers' necks or holding a fathers' hand and feel as though I am going to wretch in the middle of Target. I am here for shoes, but all I can focus on is the sounds of children giggling and asking for new toys or snacks around me.

I need to go.

As I emerge from the store and on to the main street and begin to walk robotically home, I pull out my phone. Everything in me tells me to put it away, do what I always do and completely disassociate from the fact that I am a mother. That I carried a child for nine months. That I held him against my bare chest—fed him, bathed him, slept by his side to make sure he was breathing in the night, read to him, sang to him, heard his first word, saw his first step, cleaned his knees when he fell, packed his lunches— loved him. I love him with all that I have still. I traded that for a bottle.

I'm staring at a feed of pictures of my son before I can stop myself and feel the self-hatred rising as I look longingly at his happy blue eyes and full cheeks.

"Hayden," I whisper at the phone.

He can't hear me. He has not been able to hear me. I have not talked to my son since the day before I was arrested. I promised him I would see him, instead I went to jail. No one is willing to take that chance with me again.

On Thanksgiving he had accidentally picked up my mother's phone when I called while he was playing a game. He was still new to kindergarten, couldn't read the name on the screen, but he knew it was me.

"Mommy? Mommy!"

"Yes baby! It's me." I wanted to scream, "I love you."

Instead, I bit back the urge as tears filled my eyes and my mother quickly took the phone from him. It was my first holiday without him. It wouldn't be my last.

I walk up Lake Avenue in a fury, even though the very thing I am running from is trapped within my flesh.

I try to soothe myself thinking on all of the lessons I have learned in my treatment programs. The jargon from 12-step groups or therapy isn't helping me much now, and so I try to focus on the science of it all. *The limbic system is broken in the alcoholic*, I remember, *and even more so in the mentally ill alcoholic.* That's it. My brain is broken. I cannot fathom the things I have done but that are clear as day on paper in my sober, somewhat sane mind at the moment and I wonder if perhaps it is easier when I am in my states of intoxication or loss of sanity. I want so badly to never be prisoner to either of those states either again.

I have power over the first one, I think, as I ruminate on my measly but empowering near-30 days of sobriety. As for my mind, well, I have learned it has a mind of its own, and it terrifies me.

I am close to home now and I think of the girls in my Sober Living house. Four out of seven of us have children. The others seem quite content with their situation of shared living, random hookups, and infinite gossiping about 12-step drama—their children forgotten, at least on the surface.

I wonder how I seem, without even a photo of my son on my dresser, and my consistently off-put mood and self-imposed isolation. I am not here to make friends. I am here to get started getting sober, get my life back in some senses, started in others, and finally settle into a permanent home.

Home.

I recall the judge during my second hearing, being told by the prosecuting district attorney that I had been "transient" for the past six months. I was horrified by the accusation and my lawyer quickly corrected the error, but there was a part of me, deep down, that knew it was true.

I had a place, that I had gotten all on my own, for Hayden and I, which I quickly ruined with my drinking. I lived 30 days in a treatment center. Then to Henry's. Detox. 20 more days in a treatment center. Sober Living. Henry's again. Psych ward. Mom's. Henry's. Mom's. Henry's. Detox. Henry's. Psych ward. Rehab. Henry's. Jail.

Present: Pasadena. Sober Living. How that happened, I don't know, but it isn't jail and it isn't rehab. It's the little things.

Transient (adj.): lasting only for a short time, impermanent.

When you put it that way, I think transient should be added somewhere in my name. I have been in almost constant motion from place to place since I was 17. All I want is to rest. I want a home. I want family.

When I get back to the place I shower and sleep, I avoid my roommates by immediately retreating to the bathroom in my room and I examine myself in the mirror. My makeup has been sweated off by the walk home, but I still look fresh-faced. I am dressed far nicer than I have attempted to in months, donning a gray knit sweater that frames curves I didn't used to have in a flattering way and makes me look like a woman. My blonde hair has just been touched up at the roots and frames my faces in loose, Hollywood-style curls. But my eyes do not lie.

They show the cracks, they show the seeping of my sanity, the utter fear of the things that aren't there that so often consumes me, the wild desperation that hits when I need to feel relief coursing through my bloodstream. They show the girl who was just in jail. They show the sadness.

My phone buzzes and I break from the stare-down with myself.

Jess.

Gratitude list? Affirmations? it reads.

Right. I am supposed to be sending her ten things I am grateful for a day along with an affirmation about myself. It feels trivial, it feels forced, it feels stupid, but I am on a mission to do what I am told to get done and move forward.

I am grateful. For so much. I do not feel the need to put it in a send-able list, however, but I do it nonetheless to appease the masses.

I begin:

1. *Waking up sober*—because it *is* nice to not be nursing a hangover right now, wondering where the fuck I am, what I have done, and how I am going to apologize, and my hands aren't shaking.

2. *The rain*— we had seen quite a bit of it lately, and today was clear but still smelled like it. The rain had always brought me peace. So, I write it.

3. **Hayden**— I can't get my son from my mind, and he is a natural thing to always put here. I am so grateful for him, for his smile, for his existence. I just want him back.

4. *Henry*— My other H and obvious addition to the list. I thank God for him every morning, for him saving my life, for just existing… which reminds me:

5. **Prayer**— It's something I had abandoned for years but had started again after my failed suicide attempt and became religious about in jail. My faith in God was and is restored in a way I never thought possible, and I am truly grateful for this.

6. *Mom*— I don't always put her, but today I feel inclined to with Hayden on my heart. She's put up with a lot of my shit. She gave birth to me, she held my hand while I gave birth to my son, she has sat next to me in ER beds, she visited me in jail. I appreciate her in my own way.

The list starts to become bullshit as I begin to become resentful about having to write it:

7. *Laughing*— it's better than crying.

8. New Friends— I don't really count the new people in my life as 'friends', but rather placeholders. I nod when I should and smile when I should, but I do not and have no intention of letting them in or keeping them around. This item is a crowd pleaser though, as my treatment team longs for me to socialize.

9. *Second chances*— it sounds better like this, but in reality, I am grateful for the fifth, sixth, seventh, and eighth chances I have had. The ones from my mother, the ones from Henry, and most of all the ones from God, because I should be both alone and dead in a ditch.

10. *Other alcoholics*— also a crowd pleaser, as I try to be enthusiastic about AA, but it is somewhat true, as it's nice to not be the only degenerate in the world.

I sigh with relief as I finish typing the list into the notepad on my phone and then remember the second part of her text and let out an audible groan. An affirmation. Something positive about myself. A mantra of sorts.

It seems either prideful or pitiful, depending on what you say.

I think of all the stupid things I could write:

"I am nice."

"I am pretty."

"I am a good friend."

"I am creative."

"I am smart."

"I am kind."

I want to vomit.

I keep it simple and just write: "I am resilient." Because despite what I am, this is true. I keep fighting, and somehow, I keep living, despite the fact that I question why more often than not.

I don't feel better when I have finished the task. In fact, I think my irritation has reached an all-time high for the day as I press *send*. I've been home for a total of maybe ten minutes but feel completely stifled and think I will implode if I stay much longer, so I begin to pack my things with no real destination in mind.

There is a part of me that would adore taking a train downtown and exploring the city. There is the other part of me that reminds me that trains and I do not mix. Neither do I and large amounts of people. I have a very harsh dawning that it makes total sense to end my life, that even sober I am broken and detached and probably always will be, and I begin picturing the different ways I could do it.

Not today, I think, but I can't get the image of leaping from the tops of Colorado Street Bridge from my brain. Broken indeed.

I grab my laptop and leave in a haste before I can let the darkness fester.

Leaving the house that is nothing of a home to me at all, I feel my back begin to ache from the walking I have done around town with my small bag and half of my belongings but continue forward. I want to rest. I want to sleep and not feel afraid.

I remind myself that I will get to spend the night at Henry's in two days and I hold onto just that, but there is no future in sight but my mangled mind and what feels like a tedious time loop that is really a time bomb. I know, deep down, that it will just take the right fuse to ignite it.

❧

December 20, 2019—A note before the storm

It is almost Christmas, and here is the good news folks: if I can, you too, can stop drinking yourself to death. This does not mean that happily ever after happens though. I think my life had gotten so bad that in the pit of despair, all I could hang onto was fleeting fantasies and fairy-tales. But what is real life? I don't drink myself into oblivion on a daily basis, I haven't done so for more than a month now, which is common-place for the common man but a great feat for a madwoman like me.

God did not see fit to make me a fool, and perhaps this entire dilemma would be a much easier ordeal to overcome should I have been. No, I have been blessed with intelligence, wit, and a shred of tragic wisdom—all of which can fuel genius or the most grandiose plans of chaos and despair one's mind can conceive. Yes, because there is a tumor of darkness and depression within my brain, and when I put my energy into it and let it fester, it multiplies faster than I can even hope to contain it.

And then what? You may be telling me about how your team played, what your holiday plans are, what you are planning to wear to a function—but I do not hear you, I do not see you. I smile, I nod, because I know this is socially correct—acceptable, but I am seeing something else. I see my legs dangling off Colorado Street Bridge. I see that everyone thinks I am a beautiful girl, often called stunning or gorgeous, and how opposite of that I would look with my face caved in from the impact of hitting the trees and then the ground. I wonder if I would even have a face left at all.

That would give everyone something to write home about.

I see myself drinking a handle of cheap whiskey and downing the entire bottle of antidepressants I haven't been taking and drowning and dying in oblivion. I hear them saying "it was just a matter of time," when they find my rotting body in a motel bathroom, alone.

I see my wrists slashed and emptying out the blood of my life and growing faint from the sight of it until I fall asleep for good. It would be a messy business, but not entirely shocking. It was always the first way I thought I would do it.

I see Hayden being told Mommy is an angel now and being able to know that she isn't just gone out of his life. I see Henry in pain, but one day healing, and finding the love and family he deserves. I see my mother getting nights of sleep.

What I don't see is me. I don't know what happens after any of those horrible scenes. I believe in God, but would he believe in me anymore after that? I would do it for peace, but is that what I would find on the other side?

This pain is so searing, so heavy—and so often I feel completely alone in a world of eight billion people. I have made life, and yet I feel all I do is slowly drain it from others.

Yes, those are the dark, dark machinations of the mind of Hannah Renae. Yet there also exists the childlike wonder, and with it, so many dreams—innocent and pure.

I do not want money. I do not want prestige. I do not want to live to be 105. No, when I close my eyes, and picture a snapshot of perfect happiness—it is in an immaterial location. I am in a big bed, and the sun is shining in, and the morning breeze is coming through the windows. Henry is beside me, Hayden and our children come running in, and there is nothing but peace and happiness, family. There is no noise but the sound of laughter. It is just another day. It is not perfect, but it is my perfect.

But perhaps I think in extremes. I must either have chaos or my version of bliss—maybe I ought to start exploring shades of gray. Because the truth is, that even in that perfect picture, my fucked-up head will still exist, but does it matter if I am surrounded by love? I don't know. I terrify myself, and I often wonder if I was just not made out for this world. So, I run, and so often I think death is the simplest solution. Yet, when I think of it logically, I am trying to live, so I cannot want to truly die. It is a great conundrum, and the constant war between light and dark within the confines of my skull is so, so tiresome. I want to believe, I want to hope, I want to try, I do not want to die, but I do not want to suffer like this. I do not want to be a slave to this madness.

I know I should care, should be proud that I am not knocking back bottom shelf vodka, but so many days I do think there were days when life was better when I knocked back five whiskeys and lost myself in the music. Maybe I wasn't going anywhere, but I didn't feel, and am I going anywhere now? I don't know. I am lost, but not in the music...in my head, in my horrible, horrible head. But hey, at least I'm not drinking myself to death. For whatever it's worth.

DON'T THREATEN GHOST GIRL WITH A GOOD TIME

December 26, 2019

'Twas the day after Christmas, and all through the house, it was calm, but my head was screaming.

This was supposed to be a happy time. Christmas. Henry had a new home. He had finally made it to West LA and wanted me along for the ride. Instead, I had spent Christmas evening in heaving sobs.

"This wasn't what I was expecting this week," he told me.

I am the queen of not meeting expectations, I want to tell him. *Don't you see I am a walking disappointment?* But I just apologize.

I ruminated from night until morning in the fact that my son was probably slowly forgetting who I was, that my brother was dead as dirt. These thoughts, among my other demons, creeped into the crevices of my dreams more ferocious than usual. My recent obsession with dying and death roared with a fury as I went about that morning.

I check my purse. Eleven dollars. *Fuck.* And I am going to have to go back to Pasadena soon. When, I have not decided. I feel lost. I feel like a vagrant. I feel alone. I feel scared. I want a drink. No, for the first time in a while, I *need* a drink and not to have a good time. The thought of another day, of *another week*, sounds like the grandest of orders, and I have felt this way before. It ended on a train track. I decide not to be so dramatic.

My overdose was easy before. I knew what Librium would do, and I knew that death on it would be comfortable. Death by antidepressants, I am not so sure about. I do know, however, that I am not supposed to drink on them, and with the mindset I am in now, I know that I will be getting a drink today without question.

I scurry to the medicine cabinet. I have already taken my dosage for the day but pour a pile of the pink antidepressants into my hand and decide to take two more in the meantime. As I pop them into my mouth, I hear Henry tell me we need to run to the store, and I wait for my opportunity.

It's given to me far easier than I could have hoped for as he asks me to run into the market and grab some things for him while he waits in the car. I almost have to laugh at how easily it all works out as I scan the liquor aisle in hungry anticipation.

I look at the gleaming amber bottles of finer bourbon I would like to buy. I have Henry's credit card, and I could, but there is some semblance of conscience left within me that tells me no. I will buy whatever I am going to go to hell with via my measly eleven dollars, so bottom shelf vodka it is.

I pay for his items, and then my plastic bottle of liquid poison separately and stuff it in the new purse he bought me for Christmas before I enter the car.

We return to his new apartment and I hug my bag to my right side on the elevator ride up, conscious of my secret. In just minutes I will have the bottle cap off, the plastic to my lips, the stinging of vodka going down my esophagus, and my near 40 days of sobriety in the trash—and I could care less.

These expectations that I have set for myself all come to fruition within five minutes. I don't sip—I engulf the vodka as if it is water and I have not had a drop in 40 days.

A sixth of the bottle is gone in seconds and I don't feel

much and curse my tolerance. I continue to drink and then violently brush my teeth as if that will conceal the stench of what is practically rubbing alcohol on my breath. Finally, the feeling of drunkenness begins to set in, but the numbness I was seeking is nowhere to be found, as I sit on the edge of the bathtub and thoughts of icicle eyes and red hair flood into my mind.

I take five more violent sips. I can't sit here. If I do and let the thoughts fester, I know what happens. I will be back in Alaska and then I will be completely lost and won't be able to follow through on what I have started. So instead I decide to write.

I write a massive title in bold black letters: **I HATE ALL OF YOU.** And then I stop and add three dots **...but one.** I write about how much I want to die. About how no one has listened to my plight about my struggle with madness. I wonder if this is my best attempt at a suicide note in my current state of mind. I try so hard to direct my anger towards feeling misunderstood, feeling alone, but icicle eyes haunt my thoughts, and suddenly, the North is being painted on my page and I am hitting the keys as though they are stabbing the Man with the Red Hair himself.

At several intervals I get up, drink, brush my teeth, write more, drink, brush my teeth, repeat. Henry eventually comes in and in my drunken stupor I stupidly read him what I have written and cause more pain. He says little but knows I am intoxicated, and very quickly both my pills and my vodka are gone. I sit in drunken anger until I can finally communicate the only thing I really want to.

"I really want an old fashioned," I whisper.

He has the look. The old look, of pure defeat. It makes me

sad and makes me hate myself, but I also have a wave of peace go through me, because I know what it means. He has been researching the pills I took and how long it will take them to wear off. I imagine what is going through his head, how tired he is, how tired of me he is, and I want to die more.

Yet I am right about the look and he agrees to go out. As we drive, I know I should be taking in all the new sights in this new area, but all I care about is him driving faster and getting to the restaurant so I can get my drink.

When we get to the restaurant, he orders my drink for me and saves me the embarrassment of begging for one in public. It's made with the bourbon we used to drink on the nights we would go out dancing, and as I sip it, I think of those times. How nothing was certain, but at least so much hadn't been lost yet.

We end up at a jazz bar and I want to order the strongest drink possible, which is denied to me. He limits me two drinks, and the whole time I focus on how I will be getting more as I stare at a sign written in chalk on the wall:

> *Liquor before beer,*
> *You're in the clear.*
> *Beer before liquor,*
> *Don't be a little bitch.*

It makes me laugh. I may be a complete degenerate, but I know that I can drink anyone in this room under the table.

The three drinks I have in me by 11:00 PM have produced a nice buzz, but I am not where I want to be, not even close, and as we leave, I ask Henry about getting more. We start fighting about nothing at all really as I walk away from him and into the night.

Earlier that day he had told me to never walk out after I had tried to; part of me feels like this is standing up to him in my drunken state-of-mind. He grabs me.

"Let's go," he growls. I always listen to him, but now I stare at him with eyes of defiance as I rip my arm out of his grip and begin to walk in a haste again. His arm is quickly around my waist. If anyone is watching this, we must look horrific.

"You're a bitch," he says, his brown eyes seething in anger.

I stop walking, stop fighting. *I probably deserved that,* is my first thought, and I have been called that name and worse so many times, but seeing his lips shape the word and him look at me as he says it stabs so hard.

"Fuck you," is the best response I can think of, as I try to turn so he can't see me cry, but my fight for running is completely gone and I walk with my head down back to the Cadillac.

After all of that I breach the subject of bourbon again and am swiftly denied. I know we weren't far from the house, but it begins to feel like we have been driving forever as his resounding words echo in my head.

I finger at the door of the car when a thought strikes me, and I grab the latch to the door.

"Don't," is all he says, as he sees my hand flirt with the latch.

I open it.

"Hannah."

He begins to pull off of the main road to a more residential neighborhood and I open the door further. The wind is cold and bites my skin and I feel a surge of freedom as I stick half of my body out of the car. If he is saying anything, I have stopped listening, but I doubt he is as he doesn't think I will do it. I don't know if I think I will do it. Except I do.

In one swift movement my body slams against asphalt. As I see the backlights of the Cadillac turn red and the driver's door open and Henry emerge, I raise my head and realize I am not dead—not even close. Just stupid.

He comes to me and grabs my face. I look at him. His eyes look so dark and genuine in the moonlight and echo the words he says next.

"I love you."

He's said it before, at my worst moments, and at some of our best drunken ones, but not like this. He means it. He loves me and I love him. We belong together. We were brought together for a reason, and I don't think I could do life without him, but in this moment and in the past few weeks I am wondering if I can even do life at all.

I wish so much that those words would have been enough for me to stop, to say enough, but my drunken head was still louder and not ready to hear the weight of those words.

As we drive home, I begin to feel the aching in my bones from the impact my body had with the street. With my head still screeching, I search frantically for a knife and start to type out a messy suicide note.

He had lacked to bring the box with knives to his new apartment, but there were forks, and as I feel the prongs, I decide that will do.

I emerge onto the balcony. The most beautiful part of his new living space. From the ninth floor you can see the beautiful skyline of West Los Angeles and the ocean during the day. But now it is night. The city is asleep, and I am not.

The blood on my wrist looks black in the darkness and I see it spill over the edge. I need a drink. More blood, as I can't decide if I should slash or stab. I can't decide anything at all, I can't think.

So, he decides for me at some point during the mess, and I am stopped. I don't know when he sees me, how he gets my makeshift weapon from me, and how he settles me into bed, but he does. But before dawn in the dead of night, when I wake up shaking and with a slashed wrist, I know I am not done. Because the screaming in my skull is deafening now and all of my ghosts have come out to haunt me.

I lay my hand on a sleeping Henry and feel his back rise and fall as he breathes. I wish I could wipe his memory from all of the pain I have caused. I wish I could wipe his memory of me. I wish I could wipe me off the face of the planet. I obsess over the next best thing.

It will still be several hours till I can get anything, but I have to make it until then. Let him have some peace, try to have some peace myself. This will all be over soon.

As he slumbers, unaware of my wakefulness or intent for the following day, I close my own eyes, and whisper, "I love you too."

HINDSIGHT IS 2020

If I die, it will not be in 2019, and that in itself is an accomplishment.

But it is the third day of the new year and I am scrutinizing myself in the mirror. My face is serious, but sad and scared, and I focus with intent on my own eyes.

"Don't. Be. An. Idiot," I command myself. I say it again: "Don't be an idiot."

Because to drink right now would be the most idiotic, foolish, ungrateful, and above all, cruel thing I could do. Yet, nonetheless, being who I am, I want a drink. For the past two hours I have been fantasizing about it. Thinking about the taste of a glass of fine cabernet on the beach, or a whiskey, neat, burning my throat as I listen to jazz as smooth as my drink in the background. That would be nice.

Behind me, in the reflection, is the cityscape and if I stand and turn around, I know I will see the ocean outside the window, gleaming in the afternoon sun. Henry will be home later, and all will be well. I finally have a home, a place to call my own, ours…and I want a drink.

I return to my computer and try to busy myself in work and not think of the six dollars on the kitchen counter and the spare change in my purse and the liquor stores that line the street. Because I will not be getting an old fashioned on a rooftop bar if I choose to drink. No, if I choose to drink, I will be throwing away a real chance at life, at love, at family, at home, for bottom shelf vodka and shame. The worst part is that there is a dark crevice within my brain that tells me it is worth it. I scream at it to be silent.

As I begin designing my third webpage of the day, almost robotically, it dawns on me that I am actually a skilled person. My phone call from earlier in the day implied all of the contrary, however. On paper, I am a walking disaster.

Treatment center assessments have become second nature to me. Things I could answer in my sleep. Nonetheless, they are excruciating, and as I did this one, alone and staring at myself in the mirror, I wondered if the admissions representative on the other end of the line could taste the shame in my voice.

"I was just like you," he told me.

I doubt it, I think.

"And now I have been sober four years!" he beamed.

Which is wonderful. I want that. I want that so bad. But more than anything I want to be free from this mental prison I cannot breach.

I answer so many questions I used to say no to, and so many they hope to hear no to with a simple "yes".

"Have you tried to kill yourself?"

"Yes."

"How many times?"

"Three."

"Have you been in the hospital in the past year?"

"Yes."

"How many times?"

"About 15."

"Been arrested?"

"Yes."

"How many times?"

"Once."

"Charges?"

"Still in the process, but: Drunk in public. Resisting arrest. Battery against a peace officer."

"You go girl."

Very funny. Only it's not, it's the bane of my existence.

"Ever been the victim of a crime?"

"Yes."

"Care to elaborate?"

"No."

"It says here from a previous assessment that you have a history of sexual and physical abuse—is that related?"

"As I said, I don't care to elaborate."

"Ok."

"Last time you hurt yourself?"

"Last week."

"Last time you drank?"

"Last week."

"Last feelings of suicidal ideation?"

"Today."

"How often do you struggle with that?"

"Every day."

"Are you planning to kill yourself?"

"No, I just think about it a lot."

"So passive suicidal ideation?"

"I guess."

"Sleep?"

"Poor."

"Why? Are you manic?"

"No. Nightmares."

"Oh. Yes, I see a diagnosis of PTSD."

"Yep."

"We can help you with that."

Heard that one before, but we'll see.

"Ok," I say.

"You're dealing with a lot of tough shit!" he says at the end of the hour assessment.

That's one way of putting it.

"I'll get back to you in a bit."

And he does. Returning with the news that I need a higher level of care and a price, already checked by my insurance. I have begun to see these things as quotes for my sanity. If I undergo this treatment, it will be my fifth in the past year, not counting detoxes or psychiatric facilities. I doubt it is a miracle center and I remind myself that I am the fuck up.

Eventually I choose not to respond to him at all. Because to think about insurance, six days of treatment a week, or picking a therapist at this moment, makes me want to drink even more. I return to my work and feel the resentment coursing through my veins.

Eventually Henry returns and the thought of drink and self-pity is still surging through me. He sees it immediately and so I tell him.

"If it makes you feel any better," he tells me, "I want to drink every day."

And in a way, it does. It makes me feel like I'm not a lonely degenerate.

"What if we could do whatever we wanted?" I ask him.

"We can," he tells me. "We can do whatever we want, but with consequences."

I know that all too well. However, the comment also

reminds me that we can do so many beautiful things, and I wonder what the consequence of doing right would be.

We spend the early hours of the evening along the Santa Monica Pier, and as we search after the sunset, we find that half of Southern California is too. People pack like sardines at the end of the pier to see the sun creep behind the waves.

We don't have the best view, or even a view at all really, but we end up at the pier's infamous carousel and lean on the railing next to each other. As I watch the wooden horses go up and down and see the two little girls lost in the glinting lights of the ride, I think of what magic it is to be a child, to be free, and how beautiful something as simple as a carousel is. There is a naïve part of me that wants to be on it with them.

On our way home we stop at the market and collect an assortment of things—fish, cheeses, crisps, bread, olives, ice cream. Nothing to really make a meal at all, but when we get home, we lay it all out and feast. He is across from me, music is playing, and he laughs, and the entire scene sends such a wave of peace and joy through me.

To the right of the food, I glance at the place where the ominous six dollars sits.

I could have lost this all for that, I think. And with that thought, I savor every flavor in every bite of food, every note of the music, and all that is Henry—his eyes, his walk, his smile, his voice, and his touch, as he brings me into his arms and into happiness.

I am not perfect, I am not well, but I am healing, I am loved, and I am home.

THIS WASN'T IN THE OUTLINE

January 13, 2020

On a Sunday morning, Henry holds me close, and protests me getting up from bed, until, in a lazy haze, we both rise. I begin brewing us coffee and reflect on all of the luxuries in my life.

As I see a warm stream of steaming black coffee coming from the single-brew machine in our kitchen, I think of the instant coffee crystals I used to mix with tepid water from the sink in my cell in jail.

I think of how I used to press my face to the foggy cell window, trying to see anything at all, to no avail. Or how I would lay on the fake grass in the summer sun at my last rehab, waiting for the UV rays to fry me as I sobbed for so many things, howling at the sky. Now, I look to my right and my eyes are graced by a skyline of West Los Angeles and an ocean view, but more than anything, I am in a place that I am afforded to call home.

It is serene. It is peaceful. It is mine.

The next day, I am walking up Wilshire in a haste, two wine bottles in tow. The morning has been far too much, and I realize how feeble I am as I take my first sip of cheap Merlot. My father broke me in one day. *Nothing has changed and I have gotten nothing but worse*, I think, as I see the insane look in my eyes in the full-length mirror.

I trace the fresh scars on my wrists that cover the old ones with a fragile fingernail as I return to the living room. On my trek to the local cornerstone, I also picked up a bunch of sunflowers. They have always been my favorite, but right now

I hate them. They are too bright and represent all that I am not.

I want a cigarette with my wine and ocean view. Yes, that sounds divine. I find the pack and a lighter easily, but before I retreat to the balcony, I decide to brace myself in the mirror again. I've slipped on a fitted black dress that Henry likes for when he comes home. The back opens and bares a section of my pale ribcage and hugs my hips.

I think that I have gotten more beautiful on the outside with age, which is appalling in itself, with the way I have treated my body, and inside I feel entirely like a monster.

Monsters can't be loved, I remind myself. *They are meant to be feared.*

I am hopelessly drunk. I am hopelessly spiraling again. I am hopeless.

It happens like it always does, very suddenly, as I do not go and retrieve my cigarette, but rather a kitchen knife. However, I do not attack the usual battleground of my wrist this time, bracing my dress up and making three neat slashes on my right hip. One of them is deep and long and begins spilling bright red profusely. I sigh and then I cry.

What am I doing? Why am I doing this? Again. More scars, and for what? Even in my inebriated state, I am able to consider my recent obsession with death and my own dying. We live on the ninth floor; I could jump and be done with it. I could go get more wine and take every pill in the cabinet.

The thought of any of that is exhausting though. Here I am, and the knife is already in my hand. I feel the soft flesh between my ribs and wonder what lies underneath and what monsters are made of as I walk into the knife twice and drop it, shaking.

I had seen blood splatter in movies, but I always thought it was a bit dramatic. Looking to the left though, there is a spray of red across the wall, and a pool of it already forming on the floor. Seeing myself in the mirror, I am even amazed at what I have done to myself.

Henry arrives at the building at some point and pleads for me to come down and I make no effort to clean up the streaks of blood on my legs and arms. I do, however, put on a coat.

How I get to the car or him, I do not know, and the world becomes hazy and exists in frames and flashes for the next several hours.

An ambulance ride.

An abundance of doctors staring at me as though in a dim room as though I am a fragile specimen.

Thirty-three stitches.

Henry.

Being informed that I am a danger to myself and will not be leaving the hospital under any circumstances tonight.

A warm welcome to the psychiatric unit at UCLA.

As a nurse tries to orient me to the unit, I am overcome with a fatigue that I have not felt in a very long time and beg for sleep as I feel heavy with pain medication and Ativan. I lay down in my new room, that I will inhabit for an unknown amount of time, and let slumber consume me. I dream of nothing.

The next day I am promptly seen by a whole team of psychiatric professionals who already seem to know an abundance about me and take careful time listening to my plight for release. The doctor agrees to it, hesitantly, if I can get into an outpatient program immediately, but it won't be till the next day.

I spend Tuesday staring out at unsuspecting pedestrians, who know nothing of me or my menagerie of madness. My side aches and my mind and body are weak from sedatives.

I don't even know if I was trying to die. Perhaps I was just trying to let something out, but before I knew it, they were putting me back together. I am shit at dying and as I mouth a messy, but honest prayer in the corner of my room, I wonder why God keeps me here, keeps me breathing.

I look down at the paper and pencils they have given to me. I have drawn pathetic doodles of a cat, a dog, and what is supposed to be Henry and I holding hands. My new treatment team has made several remarks about my intelligence, but as I stare at my drawings and my desperate writings, I cringe at the fact that Ativan reduces me to the brain processes to that of a five-year-old.

The doctor is true to his word though and I am released the next day.

Taking your first shower after the hospital, jail, or a psych ward always feels baptismal. I try to focus on nothing but the heat of the steaming water, the tendrils of the droplets going down my spine, the bits of course, accumulated body hair coming off of me in swift motions from the razor, the smell of coconut and hints of vanilla in my soap.

Don't look down. Because if I do, it's all right there, like a torn-up tapestry: my body. I want to cry when I see my reflection as the sunken-in quality of my eyes, the pallid tone to my skin, and my stitched-up abdomen make me look like a poorly repaired ragdoll.

My face is still pretty, I tell myself, but my body is absolutely thrashed and as I finger the curling black stitches, I know I will bear these scars for the rest of my life. So much for the perfect summer body.

When I emerge from the shower, Henry is on the phone, and I avoid the hallway that is still smeared with blood. It has turned brown from the days I was gone, and I can understand why Henry didn't want to look at it, let alone clean it.

During every conversation I have had with her since this ordeal, my mother has not failed to hone in on the call he made to her as I was hauled into the ambulance two days ago.

"He called me sobbing," she repeats, as I let her know I am home and okay. "He doesn't know what to do, none of us know what to do."

Yes, I understand that. No one wants to leave me to die, and no one wants to watch the wilting way in which I live. What they don't seem to understand is that I don't want to live this way either. I hate it and I would do absolutely anything to break free from this crushing...what is it exactly?

I stare at the discharge paper the doctor handed Henry and I on my way out.

Discharge Diagnosis:

Complex PTSD: because my trauma is layered and dynamic. Because I can't get through a 24-hour period without either a flashback or a nightmare and without avoiding people, places, or things that may hurt me, but probably won't. Because I am a prisoner to the possibilities my past has ingrained in my mind, and not reality.

Major Depressive Disorder: because almost everything that is normal to normal people has become a chore for me: getting out of bed, making a meal, taking a shower, talking on the phone. And I have tried to kill myself, several times now—I'm just really bad at it.

Agoraphobia: because leaving the house is a terrifying venture, and everything bad that has ever happened to me has been in the outside world. I was primarily housebound before this whole ordeal, but now I think I will completely contain myself to the two rooms and balcony of our apartment. That will be my world because it is safe, and I have to do everything to stay safe right now or I will die.

It strikes me that he does not include *Alcoholism*, on the list, despite my being very candid about my issues with substances during my meetings with the doctor. I ponder this.

"Things were going so well," my mother reflects on one phone call. "Hopefully you can get back to that."

"Yes, they were going okay," I reply, because they were, by my standards. I wasn't drinking myself to death, wasn't hurting myself, and wasn't in a jail cell—so things were looking up, until they weren't. "The problem is, when things get bad, I almost die."

And very soon I will die, if something doesn't change. I'm running out of lives.

She has no comment.

On the kitchen counter, I spot another paper, one that was not in the pile I had brought back with me. As my eyes quickly scan it, it becomes clear what it is: a criteria form for my 5150 hold.

Henry is still on his call, and I try to stifle my laughter as I read the blaring line in the center of the sheet.

You are being placed in this psychiatric facility because it is our professional opinion, that as a result of a mental health disorder, you are likely to: (check applicable)

[X] Harm Yourself [ ] Harm Someone Else [ ] Be unable to take care of your own food, clothing, or shelter

*We believe this is true because: **You Stabbed Yourself***

I know I shouldn't be laughing, and I think of how distorted my sense of humor has become. Yet I am shocked that this statement of intent to commit me was written by a medical doctor and find it immensely comical.

It's a true statement, but you would think eight-plus years of medical school would lead you to write something more elegant like "Self-Inflicted Laceration". I appreciate the doctor I can't remember who wrote this though, as I smile. Facts are facts. I stabbed myself, and I lived.

I decide to sit with myself and my thoughts for a long few minutes as Henry finishes his phone call, my damp hair clinging to my face.

I was really starting to let go more and more by the day as it began to feel like the light within me was slowly going out. Sitting here now, home, and welcome home, I had the pressing feeling that it was either all almost over, or perhaps everything was about to begin. One possibility gave me peace, the other scared and excited me—but I knew I had to decide.

If I chose the first option, I had quietly decided that it was only fair to prepare those who loved me for my imminent decease by letting them know, and perhaps letting them go. There was something though, there had to be, that wanted to live. It existed somewhere within me and if I wanted to live, I had to figure out what it was, and cling and claw to it until I could come up for air.

THE PERPETUAL PATIENT

January 16, 2020

The day after my release from UCLA we are headed to see good old Dr. N. The doctor who held my hand at the start of this ordeal and was still trying to walk me through it—most of the time it was pulling.

During my first visit at his private practice, as I was bringing him up to speed with all that had happened in the six months since I had seen him from my first detox he comments:

"From the moment I met you, trauma bleeds into every aspect of your life," he told me.

I reflect on this as I ready myself that morning, staring at the two massive rows of stiches along the left side of my ribcage in the mirror. Am I the traumatized or the traumatizer?

Along with my standard antidepressant and migraine

medication, I down a fistful of gummy multivitamins in one mouthful, their varying fruit flavors leaving a waxy film of artificial nutrition across my tongue. I chase the sorry excuse for breakfast with a few gulps of lukewarm black coffee.

My body feels like it is shutting down. I have hardly been able to touch food, the very sight of it sending a wave of nausea and a disgust through me. More than that, I am hurting. My bones ache, my head throbs and is dizzy, and I feel like I have been stabbed. That is because, I have been stabbed, by myself, as the doctor at the hospital put it. The more I think about it, the more the stitches in my side begin to itch.

I am too fatigued to go through the mess of my clothes and pick out the first thing that looks comfortable and will cover me—a striped, white, cotton long sleeve. As I slip it on, I mutter a prayer that my side doesn't start spontaneously bleeding on our trek out because bright red blood will seep through the bleach white of the shirt with ease and make a scene. I'm already good enough at doing that on my own. Today, I just want to hide.

I finger at my side above my shirt as we drive to Burbank. My nerves grow more uneasy as we get closer, as I feel entirely vulnerable bringing Henry with me. This is the first visit I have asked and allowed him to come to. In the past I had always tried to compartmentalize. My love and my relationship in one box, my sanity in another. Yet as my progressive breakdowns began to leak into everything, from him and I to the way I breathed and walked, I knew I either had to shut him out or let him in completely. I was terrified of the latter, fearing he might run.

This is the same man who just held you while they stitched you back together, the rational side of my head tells me. While the other side, whatever that is, screams: *He deserves better, you deserve nothing. It's just a matter of time before he realizes that.*

We arrive at the office and are greeted at the front desk by the doctor's receptionist, Daisy. She has cropped, curly brown hair that hugs her costive face. I do not particularly like or dislike her and treat her with an air of disdain today for no reason at all.

"Did UCLA call you?" I ask her, as the blood pressure cuff tightens around my bicep.

"UCLA?" she asks, cocking her head, looking perplexed. "No, they didn't. Why?"

"I was 5150'ed," I announce, and she doesn't look surprised. After all, it's me she's talking to. "Got out yesterday."

"Oh," she replies, looking down. "Well, we'll be sure to let the doctor know."

"WHY DO YOU THINK I AM HERE?!" I want to shriek, but I don't. Instead I look to Henry.

His phone is up, held vertical in both hands. He is smiling at the screen and I realize he is taking a picture. He puts the phone down.

"I was trying to get you looking away," he says. "You looked so beautiful."

I let out a half-smile, but the comment makes me want to cry. Hasn't he seen my wrist? Hasn't he the battlefield underneath my shirt? Hasn't he seen the sulking, sad, sanity-slipping disaster that is me? It baffles me that he finds anything beautiful or anything to love in the mess of these scars—both visible and deep within me. Yet he does. He always has.

There was a part of me that never trusted it—his love. There had to be something he wanted, something he was lying about, some shoe waiting to drop—but it never did. When I fell, he was always there to pick me back up and tell me that because I was still breathing, there was still hope.

I'm in love with the way his cheeks hug his brown eyes when he smiles. The way they are now how he is looking at me. It is his most genuine look. I have never seen him look this way in a photo, with a client, or even with a friend—only with me and I realize that there is nothing for him to take from me. He has only given, like he is doing in this moment, simply by existing, and I love him.

"Hannah?" Daisy says, "You two can come on back."

On our way to the back of the office I retrieve a miniature water bottle from a wicker basket, and down the entire thing in five nervous sips as we wait for the doctor. His arrival is swift, and he opens the door with his usual aura of bold boisterousness. Henry will like him. I know this already. I like him too, but I don't know if I will like what he has to say today.

I explain the past three days to him in chopped detail, letting Henry fill in the gaps, but a flash of my ribcage gives him all of the evidence he needs. The good doctor lets out an ominous sigh.

"Do you want to live?"

A good question, and one he has asked before. Do I? I think so. There are surely moments where I don't want to, but I fight them, I have fought them, I am fighting them right now.

"I think so," I say, instead of yes, because it feels more honest. "I just can't feel like this anymore, and the drinking..."

"It's not about the fucking drinking," he says, and I appreciate him so much more for using a four-letter word. "It never has been. You know that, I have told you that, another doctor just told you that. It's secondary."

Which means, it's my head. My fucked-up head. It always has been, always will be. I know this. What am I going to do about it?

"More than that," he continues, "I think you have a serious problem accepting love, accepting help. It undoubtedly stems from your childhood. Just look at you and your mother. Seeing the two of you interact is, well...strange at best. She is very stoic, and you're very closed off."

"Yeah, it's weird," Henry chimes in and I try to fight past my natural inclination to assume I am being teamed up on and listen.

"Whatever happened with your father and everything else that has happened has left some damage. You have love right here, sitting right next to you, and you can't even see it."

I say nothing.

"You've tried all of the 'bread and butter' solutions for... how long now? It doesn't matter. 12-step groups, basic CBT-therapy, group therapy, IOPs, rehab—you name it, you've done it, but you are and will continue to be a complex case and need complex care. Intensive trauma therapy, intensive cognitive interventions, and a lot of long-term work."

I nod, trying to process it all, until he asks me something that doesn't take much time to think about at all.

"Do you want your son to have to grow up having a mother who killed herself?"

I shake my head side to side right away, because no, no I do not. I then look over at Henry. His eyes are tired but understanding and locked on me. He is here and he is going to be here, accept it. I have a son who needs me. I have

Henry who needs me. I have a mom who needs me. I need me.

"Don't marry yourself to being a 'perpetual patient'" Dr. N. tells me. "Do something about it."

It's more of a warning than a suggestion, because I know very well that if I don't do something, I'm done for.

It's time to go, and for the first time in days, I feel like I can eat. We head to a diner across the street and I devour a French dip sandwich dripping in au jus. The roll the meat sits atop of is as big as my head and Henry laughs at the fact that I eat it all, but I know he is glad.

A week later, he tells me very firmly to write up an agreement. If I drink, I am gone. No arguing, no begging, no negotiating. He can deal with the rest; he just can't deal with the monster that emerges when I try to numb. I write it up in a drunken stupor, but reflect on it the next day, and feel firm about it and I cry.

I weep for all of the things that have happened, for all of the things that I have done, for the things I have seen, for the things I have said, for the things I have lost, for the things that will never leave me, for what I have given up—because for the first time, I am not arguing with myself in my head about how I am going to sneak the next bottle into the house or beg for the next escape.

The demons are coming in full force, but at least I know they are on their way, and I do not have to fight them alone. I'm done. I have to be.

I write. I write and I write about all of the things that ever hurt me until my fingers hurt instead. I awake from my nightmares and I go look at the sky and I fall back into bed and lay my hand on Henry's back and feel the rhythm of him breathing. My head is filled with a million terrible things, but there is a brief moment of respite, of a beautiful thought, that I once dreamed of this moment, of being here with him, and here it is—in my arms and I am grateful.

I listen to the small groans he makes as he tosses in his slumber the sounds of the wind and the city waking up at dawn. It is a new day, and with the freedom that I may be dealing with the madness inside my head till the day I die, but if I so choose, I do not have to deal with the aftermath of my drinking or hurting myself ever again.

It's at 5:30 AM I feel the pang of longing for my son that is normal. I am not dissociating from being a mother and I am allowing myself to hurt. It's time to do something about it.

THERE'S A FLY ON MY CHARCUTERIE BOARD

January 29, 2020

I am running, sprinting as fast as I can to get away. From what, I don't know, as my eyes are clouded in darkness, but it could be a thousand things. Yet as I am stopped by the harsh chill of the Alaskan spring morning, on my bare wet skin, I know what is behind.

I can't see what I am running from because my eyes are shut and it's as if the deprivation of my sense of sights brings all the other ones to a heightened form of life. The breeze feels like needles against my skin as it whips and stings. My mouth is dry and as barren as a desert and I taste fear on every bud on my tongue. There is an ominous wet, warmth between my legs that is in such conflict with the cold, and I can feel the shades of red. The only noise is me—but I am a symphony of panic, as the sound of my own heartbeat booms in my ears and my breathing takes on its own wild, scared song. I want to seal my nostrils from the scent of the salt from my tears, and the odor of metal that is the essence of blood.

I feel the hand on the back of my head, feel the grip tightening and pulling and I hear *his* voice.

"Where are you going, sweetheart?"

I don't answer. I don't scream, because it doesn't matter. It isn't real. What is real is that I am now awake, drenched in sweat and panting for breath, but as I look to my right and see the slivers of moonlight illuminating Henry's body rising and falling with breath. I know that I am at home and that I am safe. I may not be able to rest, at least for a while, but I can breathe.

I pace around the apartment like a madwoman for a good fifteen minutes and ponder if it is really in fact "mad", compared to the alternative. The other option being, that I numb these horrors for a minute, maybe a few days, until my temporary solution almost kills me. Suddenly, the circles I make from the kitchen to the living room are made with a much more confident gait.

I fall asleep for another short hour. When I awake again, I fall into the bad habit of not starting every morning how I promised I would: falling to my knees in thanksgiving. Perhaps there is fault in that, but I see God in other ways.

Every day I stumble in a haze from bed for good in the morning, almost always exhausted from a long night of falling asleep, waking, wrestling with my mind, and repeating the cycle until I deem that the day should begin. Before my eyes even have a chance to adjust, I am in Henry's embrace, letting the sweet lingering scent of his shampoo permeate through my nose as he nuzzles his head in my neck. The first thing I am given in the morning is love, and it is the last thing I am given at night. It is a gift, and so often I say a silent prayer in those tender moments.

I let God talk to me through the sky—as it takes on its own life throughout the day. From our balcony I can see the different ways the sun hits the ocean and makes the water dance. It is not terrifying, it is beautiful. At dusk I watch the sun fall into the sea and with it the sky turns a mood of different colors—a canvas with its own artist every night. It is then that I give thanks; it is then that I have peace.

On this morning though, something is unusual as I am up

and awake before Henry. As I let him sleep in, listening to him snore softly to the soundtrack of the beeping cars and cranes of the LA morning, I sift through my recent collection of poetry—organizing a handpicked collection I will give to him on Valentine's day.

I may be a poet, but I am not cut out for designing photo books, I realize, as I grow more and more frustrated with an online software. I give up on trying to fit pictures into pre-sized frames and give in to the rumbling of my stomach instead.

Our fridge is filled to the brim with fresh produce, and the sight of it organized neatly makes me content. Still tired, I lazily spoon heaping globs of Greek yogurt, granola, and berries into a bowl and sit alone at the breakfast bar—content in the peace and quiet of the morning. Life is not perfect, but it is better in many ways.

My breakfast is interrupted by the sound of sirens, which doesn't alarm me. We live on the busiest street in Brentwood and everything from firetrucks to police cars are constantly going up Wilshire Boulevard. What does startle me is the massive cloud of thick black smoke, like the aftermath of a volcanic eruption, through the sliding glass door. There's a fire nearby.

My gaze immediately goes to the hills beyond the boulevard but is shortened when I see a massive blaze on the balcony in the building adjacent to us. Sprinting to the bedroom without thought, my anthem in times of trouble, the most permeating word I cling onto rings out in my tone of panic:

"Henry!"

He shoots up, recognizing the sound of stress in my voice

and looks to me. What have I done now? Drink again? Taken one-too-many pills? Hurt myself? None of the above. I point at the window.

"Look!"

He looks puzzled but shifts the shutters to the left and is immediately taken aback at the sight of the fire, which has now grown into an inferno as it engulfs an entire apartment unit. Windows are shattering and debris is falling from the building.

"Oh my God," he starts, and then— "I hear screaming."

The next few hours are chaotic as people are rescued by ladder from windows or from the rooftop by helicopter. The fire grows and eats floors of the building alive and I look at the unit that is a mirror of our own engulfed in orange and black—gone.

The fire is put out, but the day brings no answers as to what or who started it. I stare at the scab in front of us: the blackened, windowless corner of a building that now taints my ocean and skyline view and I breathe. It's a good day when you really can call your issues "Cadillac problems" and the term holds true to its meaning.

However, the most permeating thing as I keep looking back at the incineration has to be the fact that I am grateful. There is a natural gratitude that I did not burn to death today. That this was not our building. That we were safe. That, unlike the residents in the building next to us, we were able to be at home tonight.

I embrace Henry and nuzzle my head into his neck. Life is crazy, life is short, and most importantly, you never know what is going to happen. The past year has taught me this more than anything, and now, here it is, a blaring reminder right in our view.

I want to tell Henry I love him, that every day with him is a blessing, but instead I let the dark part of my mind speak:

"Please don't die," I announce.

He doesn't chide me for the statement, doesn't look at me like I am insane, doesn't push me away. Instead he brings me into his arms with a touch of understanding.

"I won't," he says and it's what I need to hear. "We really need to think about fire escapes and where everything is in this building."

Good point. Preparedness. It's something I know I have to integrate into my own life to keep myself from ending up dead on the floor on any given day, to save myself from the walls of psychiatric wards, and the brick barriers of jail or prison cells.

So, I begin to try. Again. But the ten-minute journey to the place I am supposed to receive daily therapy sessions feels akin to summiting Everest.

Leave the apartment. Lock the door. Take the elevator to the lobby. Wait outside for a ride. Go straight to the building. Go to therapy. Go home. Simple enough.

I repeat this list over and over in my head as I furiously pound the elevator button to go down. I am terrified of one of my neighbors emerging from their own hovels to join me on the ride and try to speak to me. I am terrified by many possibilities—big and small—that override the simplicity of the list.

"You've experienced a lot of pain," one of my four new therapists tells me in response to my shame about the new scars on my ribcage. "Is it so bad to think that maybe you had to hurt yourself to let some light in?"

Maybe not.

I see another therapist the next day and try a different modality of treating the mountain of things that are wrong with me. Today is dialectical behavioral therapy. I immediately impress the therapist by telling her about my knowledge of the treatment and its usefulness for Borderline Personality Disorder—my mother's favorite thing to diagnose me with.

I used to resent her for this. Try and throw the diagnosis right back in her face, but now I see her point. My insurance company has been billed with a menagerie of said diagnoses, some more resounding than others—major depression, generalized anxiety, Bipolar II, complex post-traumatic stress disorder, anorexia, opioid dependence, alcoholism, agoraphobia, borderline, panic disorder—and probably a few I don't know about. I just call it "fucked up".

Today we focus on my "black and white" thinking. Because everything is either going to be terrible or wonderful, and don't tell me otherwise.

After every therapy session I rush out of the building before anyone has a chance to talk to me and order an Uber straight home. I am only finally able to feel at ease as I am enveloped by the warm air of the living room and my ears are graced by the sound of the door locking behind me.

Sprawling out on the floor, I take a breath in and wonder if things will ever be okay.

I remember then, so clearly, the day of Zak's funeral. My other half-brother's father walking up to me. Losing a sister himself many years ago, he knew my pain.

He didn't ask me what was wrong or try to tell me my brother loved me. Instead he let me sob as we stared out at the bay—my own father long gone after waving me off and leaving me in a fit of tears by the headstones.

"I'm not going to lie to you and tell you it gets easier," he told me. "It just gets different."

His words have held wise and true throughout these months as grief has taken on many shapes. Yet now, pulling at the fibers of my carpet, I am beginning to think they apply to many aspects of my life.

I will always struggle with this thing, no matter what you name it. No matter where I go, what I become, or who I am with—the noise so loud in my brain that it often feels like it is on fire. Yet I find hope in small moments of respite and I cling to them.

Perhaps true happiness is in the small hours of the night, when fear festers and you can turn, and there is someone you love to hold onto. Or it is the simple, but grand privilege of having food on the table and smiling at eyes that have gotten you through the worst times, and that you want to see you at your best, for the rest of your life. Some days, it is a mother's fatigue, but forgiveness for all that she has seen, because she just wants her daughter to live. On the days where I truly want to give in, it is the hope that despite months and miles of separation, my son still holds me in his heart, and whispers my name into my mother's ear with love and longing—and the hope, and possibility that he can, and will, be in my arms again one day, and one day very soon. Finally, perhaps it is just drawing breath, and that there has to be a reason why.

Today I choose to keep drawing life-giving air.

I pop a Kalamata olive in my mouth and remind myself silently that shit could be worse, as I stare out at the ocean view I couldn't have once imagined.

AND YOU THOUGHT WE WERE DONE

January 31-February 10, 2020

Gasping for air—chest heaving, caving in and then expanding to its full surface area. The area under my eyes is raw and I am clawing at my flesh or the wall, as I feel like my tears will drown me. They will not stop. Every time I try to soothe myself during this fit and the heavy sobbing minimizes into whimpering, something else seizes me. A painful memory, a stark reality about the present, a line from the list of self-hatred, or something that has not, may not come to pass, but has the chance to. No matter which rabbit I pull from the hat, it is mangled, bloody, and monstrous.

After an hour that feels like a year, I am able to free myself from the confines of the top right corner of the bed and I stumble out of the bedroom to the living area. The tears are still falling but are at a trickle as my despair turns to rage.

At the end of an endless January I had stopped trying to die, and simply didn't care if I did. That is what happened January 31st, as I flirted with death yet again.

I am confused as I awaken in a hospital room and not an ER bed in a place I don't know. I am alone and can taste the aftermath of the six-dollar fifth of vodka I bought in my mouth. My head spins in tune with the downward spiral I am on. As I try to get up, I immediately feel the intense rush and pulsating of blood throughout my body. My chest feels like it is going to break and the rapid beeping that spills into my ears from the heart monitor sends a shock of anxiety through me.

I decide against sitting myself up but wince in pain as I feel a sharp sting shoot through my left wrist and grab for it. My right hand feels the stitches before I see them. A memory registers.

My wrist was a river of red. The bright crimson had sprayed all over the bathroom—the mat, the porcelain countertops, the edge of the shower, the walls.

I was trying to get something to stop it, a makeshift tourniquet for another drunken violent act against myself. And then?

Somehow, I had gotten here. Meaning he had found me. Sobs begin to rack through me as I have muddy flashes that are hardly memories of doctors and hospital staff surrounding me and screaming—my screaming.

A week later I am staring at myself in the mirror of a dingy psychiatric hospital in Torrance. I have written a letter to an unknown board of psychiatric professionals who will decide if the 5250, 14-day hold my doctor has put me on has enough merit.

I haven't had a stitch of makeup on in days and my hair has all of the Irish frizz and curl I try so hard to vehemently flat iron out every day. I am clad in baby blue pajama bottoms that are freckled with Christmas trees, a black sweater, and lime green hospital socks. My skin is dry, cracked, and broken out as it is still expelling the bottom shelf liquor I consumed over a week ago. Most predominant though, is that with everything shed, the forest green of my eyes strikes through everything and I look so young. I stare at a child begging its own reflection for a reprieve and finding nothing.

I find solace in the fact, that despite this sight, I have my most fierce weapon, my most faithful companion, and my strongest advocate—my words. They are strong, they are smart, they are evocative, they are true, and they are mine. Despite all that I have lost, nothing has been able to snatch this pen from me.

I walk into my hearing with a half-confidence that hangs solely on my words. My social worker wastes no time reading my list of sins.

"Hannah has a history of suicide attempts, a recent one in August involving train tracks."

"Hannah has current pending legal charges for assaulting a police officer. Her most recent hearing was January 24th, and is contributing to her depression"

"Hannah has been hospitalized three times in the past month for self-harm related incidences while under the influence of alcohol."

It was only twice, I almost say, but hold my tongue, as I realize this is not much of a defense.

"Hannah has been in residential care three times in the past year and has had multiple failed attempts to get and stay sober."

"Hannah has been withdrawn and has not been participatory in groups since her admission at the hospital and has failed to connect with both her peers and treatment team."

I stop hearing what she has to say and bite my cheeks—as I cannot decipher if I will burst into tears or rage. The familiar, compulsive need to shriek is searing throughout me. I feel like bursting into a monologue of explaining myself to the librarian-looking woman who sits across the table from me, jotting down everything the social worker says. She will decide my fate.

I ignore the social worker's prosecution of me completely and stick to my plan and read the letter. I touch on the nature of my mental illness and my responsibility in its progressive spiral, the fact that I understand the seriousness of my condition and my recent behaviors, that I am not like the homeless, displaced folk who they call "my peers" here. I live in Brentwood for God's sake, and I have a loving partner who is supportive of my recovery. I heavily focus on the fact that I will be seeing my doctor immediately upon discharge, ignoring the comment by my social worker that I have refused a fourth residential treatment center. It's Hannah's way or the highway, and I am going home today. I am having caffeinated coffee. I am having a cigarette. I am having a good meal, and I am having Henry. Today.

Only I am not, because while my letter is, in the librarian's words "very well-written", it is not enough to discount my recent hospitalizations and the extreme instances of self-harm. There is enough reason to keep me and I will be staying for the weekend at the least. That's that.

I submit myself to the fact that like it or not, I will be here until Monday and meander over to the sad single shelf of books the unit has to offer. Amongst a collection of airport romance novels, whose titles I don't even bother to read, I spot a black book with a red title on its spine: *Harry Potter and the Sorcerer's Stone*.

I had never been allowed to read the Harry Potter books as a child or anything like them and I cannot remember the last time I read a book meant for adolescents. Nonetheless, as the book stares back at me, it feels like God telling me it's okay. That if I am damned to hell, it won't be for reading a book about a boy on a flying broomstick. I pick it up and read through it in a few hours between suckling on nicotine lozenges and the resentment of the cigarette I won't be having today. It is difficult to digest the content as I spend more time thinking of how ridiculous it was that this is what my father worried about, as opposed to exploring the wizard world.

On my last night at the hospital, I finally discover the thing that is louder than my head—the screams of others. It is a menagerie of yelling, utter nonsense, confused rage, directed anger, and pent up violence. They are coming from every corner—the children's ward, down the hall, across the hall, and in my own room as my roommate shouts obscenities at the ceiling. If one starts another quickly begins the lament again in their own tune.

I do not hate them. I do not mourn the hours of lost sleep. This just is. I soak it all in like a sponge, discerning every noise and putting a name to it.

Yet in the short breaks of silence I am utterly with myself, and any pause in the noise makes my own thoughts so loud that it feels like my entire body is spinning. My fingernails claw at the insides of my hands and I flex my wrist in a back-and-forth motion—the newly scarred area stretching and stinging with each pull. All sensations to remind me that I am alive, that I am here, that this is now.

For the first time in a very long time, the fear of death seizes me—a terror so strong that it propels me back to an innocent, but lucid state of mind. A younger, untainted version of me trembles at the idea of an end, of what comes after, and of hell. I do not want to survive any longer, I do not want to be dragged through life.

"It's the same story, Hannah," Henry had told me on a call earlier where he had sounded like I had drained the last bit of life from him.

"You are begging and crying to get out, and you will very soon."

"I'm so sorry," I interrupt him.

"Stop saying that!" he snaps, but he doesn't follow it with the fact that the statement is meaningless or that it will just be more of the same when I get out. Instead, very matter-of-factly he states: "You are going to die."

Because at this stage, recovery has taken on a whole new meaning. It isn't about a 30-day rehab, a magic pill, or a certain number of 12-step meetings anymore. It's about living or dying—that is what it starts and ends with.

Having one foot in the grave and the other in recovery has been like standing in quicksand—and the reaper's pull is becoming more dominant. I have the sickly feeling that I have pulled the revolver too many times and that the next shot will be the one with the bullet. I can picture my mother and Henry planning my funeral in a few days' time in a very clear mental image:

My mother gray, alive but lifeless, and the flesh beneath her eyes sunken in—the ruin of the rest of her life just beginning. Henry's cool collection coming apart at the seams, coming home to the space I used to lay every night and knowing I will never be there again. Most of all, the five-year old boy who is the spitting image of me having to learn what death is at far too young an age.

And me—cold and hard, but my prepared pristine for the ground. Whatever part I have sliced too deep covered and concealed. My eyes shut and never to be reopened. My mom had said Zak looked like he was sleeping when she saw him dead. Is that how I would appear? Asleep? At peace? Or just a tragic ending in a wooden box? No parent, husband, or friend to be buried next to.

Nausea consumes me, but I assure myself that this is a good thing, because I do not want Henry's words to come to pass. I want to live—for these scars to be nothing more than spilled ink on a masterpiece.

I walk free from the doors of the hospital at noon after twelve long days and fall into Henry's arms in the lobby. Everything around me, except for him, is too saturated and I hide in a blanket from the world until I get my long-awaited cigarette-after-captivity.

Only it doesn't taste like heaven, it has no flavor of freedom— it makes me sick. I struggle to get through half of it as I can barely stomach the blaring sunlight, the noises of vehicles around me, and most of all, the stark realization of how pathetic I look and feel. I stumble back to Henry's car in a fit of shaking and sobs. I am a mess. An utter, petrified mess.

He doesn't have to ask me what is wrong—he knows and without question he cradles my head on his chest. I breathe in the smell of his Tom Ford cologne that is so much sweeter than concoction of ashtray, stale soap, sweat, and tears I must reek of.

"You are safe," he assures me.

I nod silently and clutch him like a life preserver.

"Where are you?" he asks me.

"With Henry," I say, and that is home.

CALIFORNIA DREAMIN', MY HEAD IS STILL SCREAMING

March 2020

It's a good day, a perfect day. I'm on Santa Monica Beach. The sky is blue as can be and the waves sing a gentle song as they coast into the shore. Coming straight towards me is my son, shovel and pail in hand—his smile beaming. Before he reaches me, I feel the embrace of the arms that have become home take a hold of me and I fall back into the sand laughing.

"I think your mom wants to go for a swim," Henry says with a smirk as he begins tugging my hand.

I half-heartedly fight the pull, knowing I am going to end up in the water, and within seconds the scene comes to pass as I trip into a dip in the sand and fall into a wave. As I emerge from the saltwater and fling the wetness from my hair, my ears are filled with the serene sound of the two people I love the most laughing.

As I flee from another wave and back to the sanctuary of our umbrella, it is hard to miss the sunlight illuminating the diamond on my left hand. The light refracts beautiful rainbow colors from the gem and it completely draws any attention away from the faded, now-silver scars on my wrist. It is hard to believe that I was ever the girl on the train tracks, in the jail cell, in the psych ward. Maybe happily ever-after's do exist…

Only, this scene is only as real as the nightmares I have—as it is just a dream. It is not happening, nor has it happened. My days do not paint this picture, but there are so many beautiful brushstrokes when I look for them.

On a Monday, my life looks like this:

Most of the city is at work; I am at the beach where my fantasy has not yet and may never be fulfilled, but Henry is with me today. As is his cousin, Eddie, who has just completed a year in residential treatment for dancing with the same demons I have.

Eddie and I are nothing alike on the surface. He is brown, I am white. He is big, I am small. He is in his mid-30s, I am pushing 23. His eyes are kind and relaxed, mine are watchful and afraid. But we are the same—and the fact that we are here, under the winter sunshine that paints the water a thousand shades of blue—is nothing but a miracle.

We have both been prisoners to the madness the mind can play. We have both been dragged to the gates of hell at the end of a pipe or a bottle. We have both had to call a jail cell home for a time at one point in our lives. But here we are. Free, smiling, and most importantly: alive.

The water is cold that day, but I let it hit my knees and feel its energy surge through me. I no longer fear the lake, or the things of the North, or things unknown—for I have braced the depths of the ocean.

The water makes me think of Zak and of things lost, but the freedom I have to walk in and out of the tide also reminds me of all the things to be gained.

Tomorrow I have an appointment with Dr. N. for my fourth Ketamine infusion. I don't know if it is working or helping, but something is, as even though the darkness still seeps into every day, I am able to see the light a little brighter. Like right now, as I see the sunrise in the brown of Henry's eyes as he beams at me on the beach. This is the best gift I can give him—me living and me living well. My story has just started, as has ours.

My scars become a bright purple as my skin grows cold and goosebumps rise on my skin—but I do not mind. Scars mean that the healing is happening. For whenever I need a reminder that I have made it and will continue to make it, all I need do is look at the tapestry of my skin. Stretch marks, tattoos, and scars create a canvas on my flesh, marks of life that tell the true story. Yes, I've put the things that sear into stanzas and into these pages, but the real narrative screams through every single one of these tiger stripes—the ones on my body and the ones that live deep within me. They knit me together, they keep me living, and they push me forward.

I have yet to see my son. Henry and I are still healing. The scars on my body permeate through my snow-white complexion and remind me that I am not far from where I just was. The thought to end my life comes without fail every single day, sometimes several times. But it is just that—a thought, and my will to live, and my belief in miracles is much stronger.

Fairytale endings were not written for warriors' journeys and stories such as this, because to win a war like this you have to battle every day. Sometimes you'll get hurt, and more often than not, before it gets better, it will get worse, but if these things that sear through these pages could scream, they would say this:

"Look at how far you have already come. Now keep going."

I am not where I want to be, but I've stopped defining a place of where I should be. Because the true hope lies in the fact that these pages are complete and that you are reading these words. I will not lie and say that it gets better, but if you hang on, it does get different, and you learn to live with what you are given in a way that works.

If it has existed in me, I believe it exists in everyone—that capacity to be brave enough to keep walking forward and face the gates of hell square in the eye and say: "not today." The faith to believe that if you draw breath, God deems you deserving and will keep your heart beating when facing the day feels as daunting as the depths of the ocean. And the courage to lean on the ones who love you when walking feels too hard but doing absolutely anything to put one foot in front of the other.

I do not wish these things that I have and continue to see, feel, and be on anyone, because the word for the way I live is simply this: *haunted*. My brain is so loud that sometimes it feels like it is on fire. Yet, I find hope in my moments of respite, however small or large they tend to be.

Most of all, I am refusing to die, even on the days when living is agonizing. The waves come and sometimes they wash away the castles I make out of sand, but at least I am not alone on the beach. For that fact alone, there is an abundance to be grateful for.

Perhaps some will think I should have written this story at a different time, a later time. But this story is now at an end because so is the chapter of darkness that has brought it to life. A new story is for a different book and for a different woman to tell—this has been the journey of how she was broken to be reborn before she could truly live.

If you or someone you love is struggling,
please call the
National Suicide Prevention Lifeline at
1-800-273-8255

DID YOU ENJOY THIS BOOK?

You can help make a difference for the author by showing your support!

Reviews are the most powerful tool in an author's arsenal when it comes to getting attention for their books. Honest reviews help bring the attention of other readers and spread the word so more people can enjoy the stories authors have to tell.

If you enjoyed this book, please consider taking a minute or two to leave a review on any of your sites.

We appreciate your support!

ACKNOWLEDGMENTS

Writing has always and continues to be my dream. The story in this book was by no means the kind of book I thought I would ever publish—but I am proud that I did. *Tiger Stripes* was born out of what was truly the most painful period of my life, but I think the fact that it is exists and that I am writing this now, happy, healthy, and very much free from many of the demons that once haunted me—shows just how much hope there still is in the world. I have so much gratitude in my heart for anyone who has read my story.

To those who have followed along and watched me grow in my sobriety from afar and supported my writing far before the publishing of this book—thank you so much. Your support has pushed me to continue to recover, continue to share my experience, and continue to tell stories.

I cannot express enough thanks to my publisher. I feel beyond fortunate that I found Hurn Publications and am grateful that I have had Meaghan to guide me through the entire, sometimes messy process of publishing a book. I relapsed four days before she told me she was willing to take a chance on the story and have been sober since. Someone telling me that my story was worth telling was one of the catalysts I needed to keep on living at a really dark time. I am so grateful that her and Rae helped me tell my story in a way that is raw, real, and true to all that I experienced.

I am thankful for all of those who inspired my recovery:

1. My son: I'm finally happy to say I have this beautiful little boy back in my life and the opportunity to be a mother to him is one of the greatest gifts and reasons for me to keep going even when the going gets rough.

2. My mother: Though we haven't always seen eye-to-eye, my mother has unfailingly believed in me and been there at some of my darkest moments. I am so thankful that I still have her in my life and that I have the relationship I now do with her.

3. Zak: It's been almost two years since my brother has been gone and it still is the most painful thing to think about. I often find myself looking at many of the last things he sent to me and reminiscing on some of our last conversations. I know he would be so proud of this book and me though and that gives me some peace.

Finally, perhaps it goes without saying, but I could not have done any of this without my dearest Henry. He has held me at my worst, cheered me on at my best, and been there for everything in between. He pushed me to write this story and to begin healing when all I wanted to do was continue down a path of darkness. That push didn't just give me my life back, it gave me an entirely new freedom and sense of purpose I could have never imagined—I am so glad I get to experience it with him.

I hold the second chance I have been given more sacred than anything in my life. I hope my experience has shown that no one is condemned, and everyone has the opportunity to recover.

"Even the darkest night will end and the sun will rise."-Victor Hugo

ABOUT THE AUTHOR

If there is anything Hannah believes in, it's hope, but that wasn't always the case. For a long time, chaos was comfortable for Hannah, but at just 22 she would have to make her hardest decision yet: was life really worth living?

Since picking up a pen Hannah has had a love for writing, and as an adult it would become her greatest tool in healing from an almost decade-long battle with severe mental illness and substance abuse. Her first book, Tiger Stripes, is a harrowing, raw telling of her year in and out of hospitals, treatment centers, and jail that finally led her on the road to recovery and freedom.

Hannah was born in Orange County, CA but has lived in the Los Angeles area for several years. She now lives in West L.A. with her boyfriend. When she is not writing she can be found reading, running, cooking, or finding the best vegan eats in L.A.!

Connect with Hannah:

www.hannahrenaeauthor.com

On Instagram: @hannahrenaeauthor

On Twitter: @byhannahrenae

BOOK CLUB QUESTIONS

1. What was your initial reaction to the book? Did it hook you immediately or did it take time to develop and bring you in?
2. Do you think the story was plot-based or character driven?
3. What was your favorite quote/passage?
4. What made the setting unique or important? Could the story have taken place anywhere?
5. Did you pick out any themes throughout the book?
6. How credible/believable did you find the narrator? Do you feel like you got the true story?
7. How did the characters change throughout the story? Did your opinion of them change?
8. How did the structure of the book effect the story?
9. Which character did you relate to the most, and what was it about them that you connected with?
10. How did you feel about the ending? What did you like, what did you not like, and what do you wish had been different?
11. Did the book change your opinion or perspective on anything? Do you feel different now than you did before you read it?
12. The book is being adapted into a TV series, who would you want to see play what parts?
13. What is your impression of the author?
14. Who is your favorite character and why?
15. If you could meet one of the characters right now, what would you say to them?

MORE FROM THE AUTHOR

Coming March 2022
The Way She Burns

Enjoy a collection of the artists poetry in both printed and
spoken form.
The book will be released in eBook format only to allow all
readers the chance to see the video performance of poetry by
the author Hannah Renae.

View more of her works on Instagram:
@hannahrenaeauthor

Turn the page to see some of her poetry!

Emancipate the words
the world has told you
belong like screams underwater.
Sisters, daughters, mothers—
we are the healers and the fighters.
We fly on the wings
of women like iron.

@hannahrenaeauthor

21st century pharisees
gave me motion sickness
from trying to shake the
red hot poetry and radio jams
out of my virgin body.
I like my music loud,
my literature obscene.
and my love like sunshine—
I crave kisses like morning coffee.
I'm a sad child and a weary woman
but I'm *rich rich rich!*
I run towards the western sun
at twilight and I slumber
without guilt at dawn.

I sleep ok for now
and my kisses are as old fashioned
as the vanilla malts I like:
I can't keep up with the soul cycle disciples
over in Rodeo Drive paradise.
I am unremarkable, porcelain longing,
begging for the hollow space
to be filled with
something other than
the ghost of Allen Ginsberg.
If you want a home-cooked love poem
you know where to find me
and my bad jazz music.

@hannahrwcauthor

INTERVIEW WITH THE AUTHOR

Hannah, thanks for being with us today. Congratulations on your upcoming novel! We're excited to jump into this interview, so let's get to it!

Tell about yourself in a few sentences.

I am an author, poet, and mental health advocate in West Los Angeles, CA. After being dragged to the brink of death by severe mental illness and alcoholism, I have turned my pain into power and am using my voice to bring awareness to mental health issues and art as a coping mechanism.

Do you have any formal education, credentials or honors you'd like to share? We love giving authors an opportunity to show off.

- English Literature
- UC Santa Barbara (Magna cum laude)

Speaking of showing off, do you have bragging rights on anything that you'd like to share?

I got my bachelor's degree by 20 years old!

Why do you I write. Is there a philosophy behind the words?

I write to feel, heal, and process my own feelings and to better understand others.

Can you share with our readers what your favorite books are and why they're on your list?

Crime and Punishment (Fyodor Dostoevsky is one of my favorite authors for both his style and philosophy. He inspired my great love for Russian literature, and I reference him frequently in my work).

Can you tell us a little about your writing style?

I strive to create immersive scenes for my readers where I draw them off of the page and into the setting I have written. I write very raw, emotional, and often dark pieces that I believe give a glimpse into the way I feel and process life with mental illness.

What's your writing process like?

I almost always begin writing out thoughts or ideas by hand first. I will work with rough outlines for chapters, but in general I like to just let my pen (or keyboard) flow and write what I feel. I will usually go through several editing processes depending on the length of the work before I am finished.

What are you working to accomplish?

I hope that my work shows others that healing can take place from even the worst depths of darkness. I also eventually hope to provide avenues for youth and young adults to process trauma through creative outlets as I have.

Do you have any Works-In-Progress?

I am currently working on a poetry collection and just getting back to working on fiction.

Anything else you'd like to let our readers know about you?

When I'm not writing or working, I absolutely love running, cooking, and exploring Los Angeles!

ABOUT THE EDITOR

A New Look On Books
Raven Eckman, Editor

Raven is a freelance editor by night and fangirl at every other available opportunity.

She always knew books were her passion, well after her grandmother's challenge to read a book a day and obtained her B.A. in English with a concentration in Creative Writing from Arcadia University.

Currently, she is drowning in her TBR list, revising her second WIP, and expanding her freelancing business-all while looking for more bookish things to get involved with.

She is active on Twitter, Instagram and sometimes Facebook when she remembers.

Editor Links:
   Website: https://anewlookonbooks.com/
   Twitter: @rceckman
   Instagram: @anewlookonbooks

ABOUT THE BOOK DESIGNER

Triumph Book Covers
Diana TC, Designer

Diana Toledo Calçado, better known as Diana TC, was born in 1996 and grew up in Azores, Portugal.

She has been heavily influenced by her artistic family and has studied multiple forms of art while growing up, from metal embossing to traditional ceramic tile painting.

She now freelances full-time creating book covers, specializing in the genres of Fantasy, Paranormal, Romance, and Suspense. She also works on original illustrations, fine art, and writes her own novels during her free time.

Designer Links:
Website: www.triumphbookcovers.com
Facebook: @triumphcovers

ABOUT THE PUBLISHER

Hurn Publications is the proud publisher of great writers and gifted storytellers, beloved books and eminent works.
We believe that literature can fuel the imagination and guide the soul. There is a book on our shelves for every reader, and we relish the opportunity to publish across every category and interest with the utmost care, attention to diverse inclusion and enthusiasm.

Paperback: 978-1-7364509-0-1
Ebook: 978-1-7364509-1-8
Library of Congress Control Number: 2021930757
Second Edition: April 2021
Edited by: Raven Eckman of A New Look On Books
Book Cover Designer: Diana TC of Triumph Book Covers

Hurn Publications | Temple, TX www.hurnpublications.com

CPSIA information can be obtained
at www.ICGtesting.com
Printed in the USA
FSHW010803030321
79074FS